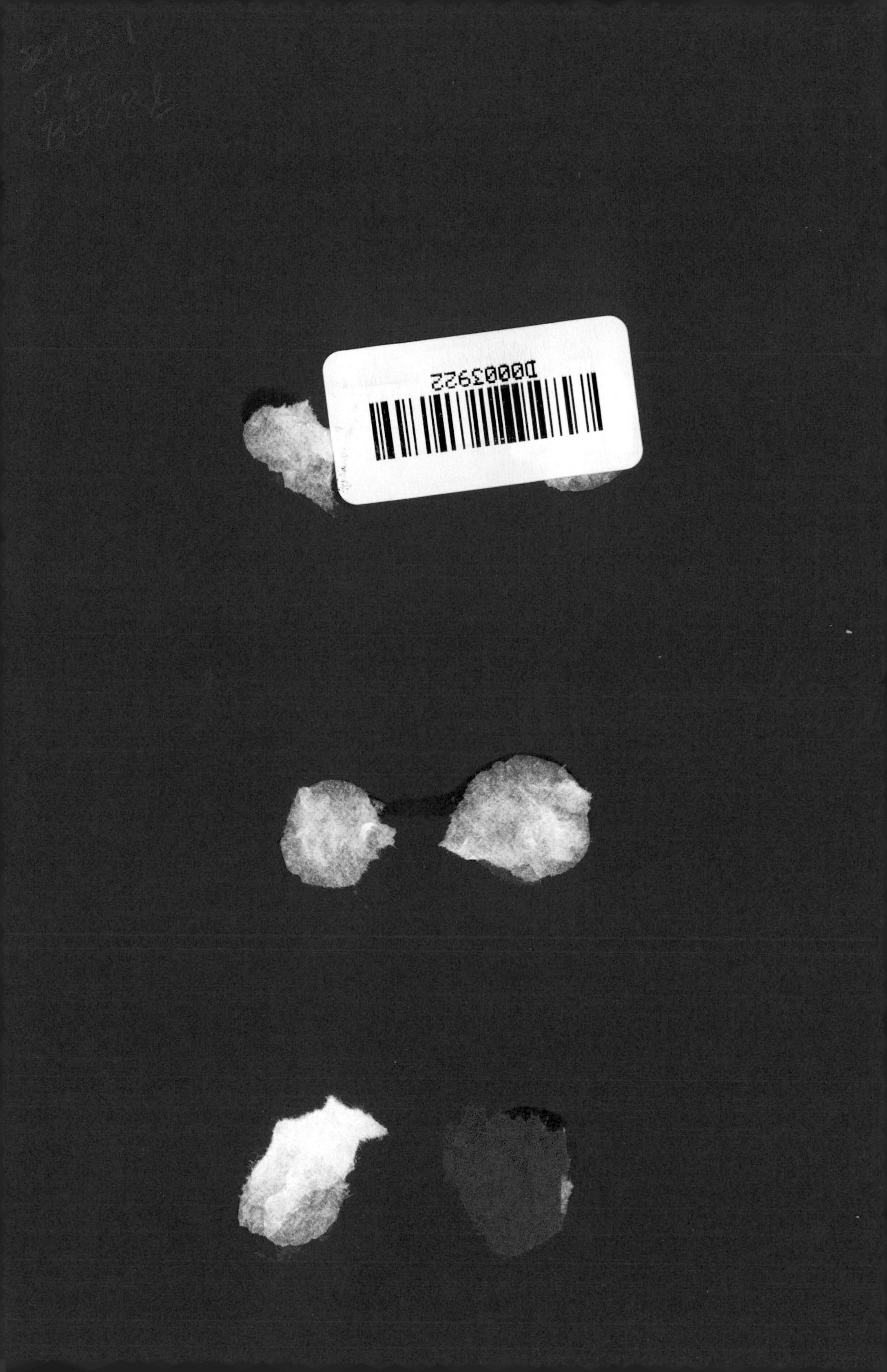

The Legend of Job in the Middle Ages

The Legend of Job in the Middle Ages

Lawrence L. Besserman

Harvard University Press
Cambridge, Massachusetts
London, England 1979

Printed in the United States of America

Publication of this book has been aided by a grant from the Andrew W. Mellon Foundation

Library of Congress Cataloging in Publication Data

Besserman, Lawrence L 1945-
The legend of Job in the Middle Ages.

Bibliography: p.
Includes index.
1. Job, the Patriarch—Legends—History and criticism. I. Title.
PN687.J62B47 809'.351 78-14936
ISBN 0-674-52385-7

For Jane Trigère Besserman

Acknowledgments

FOR GUIDANCE in the early stages of my work on Job I am indebted to Professors Morton W. Bloomfield and Larry D. Benson of Harvard University. Without their criticisms and encouragement, the way into the complex, far-flung, and long-lived legend of Job would have been very dark and forbidding. I wish to thank Professor Donald R. Howard of Stanford University, who recommended a number of revisions that have improved the book considerably.

A 1976 Summer Stipend from the National Endowment for the Humanities enabled me to spend several uninterrupted months revising my manuscript and exploring the iconography of Job. To the staff of Widener Library, Harvard University, to the staff of the British Library, and to Professor Rosalie B. Green, Director of the Princeton Index of Christian Art, my thanks for prompt and knowledgeable assistance in obtaining relevant materials.

I am grateful also to Mrs. Jesse Iarrobino, who typed the manuscript, and to my sister, Dr. Perle S. Epstein, who gave generously of her time to help read proof.

At every stage of my work on this book my wife, Jane Trigère Besserman, has helped in ways too numerous to list.

L.L.B.
Jerusalem
June 1978

Contents

Illustrations

The Legend of Job in the Middle Ages

Introduction

Who names not now with honour patient *Job*?
Milton, *Paradise Regained*, III, 95

WITH ROOTS DEEP in the cultural soil of the Ancient Near East, the legend of Job has flowered and borne fruit in almost every phase of Western intellectual and imaginative life. Its influence on our vocabulary and our stock of proverbs and proverbial phrases is marked: "the patience of Job," "curse God and die," "man is born unto trouble as the sparks fly upward," "I am escaped with the skin of my teeth," "gird up now thy loins like a man," "behemoth," "leviathan"—these are just a few of many familiar expressions from the great King James version of the Book of Job, and they have their equivalents in French, German, and other European languages.[1] No wonder people speak of Job with automatic reverence—even when they are not fully aware how central or perplexingly varied is his image in Western tradition.

My goal in this book is to trace the development of the Job legend in the course of its wanderings from its Near Eastern home and to discover how it was reshaped and recreated in the Middle Ages. My approach is primarily analytic and taxonomic, not encyclopedic. Though I have cast a wide net, this is not a *catalogue raisonné* of all the allusions to Job in the Middle Ages. Compiling such a catalogue would be like trying to draw out the leviathan with a hook, only less exciting. I have chosen instead to treat, besides the Hebrew and Greek versions of the Book of Job and the apocryphal Greek *Testament of Job*, representative medieval texts in Latin, Old and Middle English, and Middle French. Many works on Job in other (but by no means all) medieval languages are referred to in the notes.[2]

There are a number of puzzles in the history of the story of Job from biblical times through the Middle Ages that I have attempted to solve. To begin with, how did Job acquire his proverbial reputation for patience and piety when in the Book of Job he says: "Have I the strength to wait / What end have I to expect, that I should be patient?" (6:11), and when he himself impugns God's justice in a series of statements, of which the following is typical:

> I am sickened of life;
> I will give free rein to my griefs,
> I will speak out in bitterness of soul. /
> I will say to God, 'Do not condemn me,
> but tell me the ground of thy complaint against me. /
> Does thou find any advantage in oppression,
> in spurning the fruit of all thy labour
> and smiling on the policy of wicked men?'
>
> (10:1-3)

And if, as many scholars have assumed, the theological aim of the Book of Job was to discredit the view that suffering comes as punishment for sin, and prosperity comes as reward for righteousness, then why does the story end with a lavish bestowal of material rewards on the vindicated sufferer? Why is Job so often portrayed in the Middle Ages as a prophet of the afterlife, when according to most scholars there is no explicit mention of the afterlife in the Book of Job? And how did Job come by his traditional role in medieval poetry and iconography as a prophet or antetype of Christ? Or by his role as a warrior? Furthermore, though it is not too difficult to account for the veneration of Job in the Middle Ages as a patron saint of lepers, syphilitics, and melancholiacs, how was it that Job came to be portrayed as the patron saint of musicians? Why is he often portrayed as a paragon of hospitality? And where do the opinions that the Book of Job is an epic or drama originate? Finally—to step for a moment beyond the chronological limits of this book—what basis is there in the Book of Job or in other early monuments of the

Job tradition for the Renaissance view of Job as a Stoic philosopher? Or for the nineteenth- and twentieth-century view of Job as a righteous rebel against a cruel God?

These are the major avatars of the figure of Job, and they reflect the complexity of the Job tradition as well as its viability. The various stages in the growth of the legend of Job resemble a series of transparent overlay drawings. If we lift the sheets one at a time, we can see the lineaments of each more clearly and can assess its place in a composite picture that has been thousands of years in the making.

As we shall soon discover, there are three traditions in the history of the Job legend: biblical, apocryphal, and ecclesiastical; and their point of conjuncture is medieval vernacular literature (chapter 3). By "biblical tradition" I mean the Hebrew and Greek versions of the Book of Job and explicit allusions to Job in Ezekiel, the Book of Tobias, and the Epistle of James. For the "apocryphal tradition," the pseudepigraphal *Testament of Job* is our principal witness. Other versions of the Job legend that also fit under this rubric are found in Jewish and Moslem sources, in medieval art, and in medieval Latin and vernacular literature. By "ecclesiastical tradition" I mean exegetical or liturgical uses of Job. The primary texts of this tradition are Gregory the Great's *Moralia in Iob* and the Latin Office of the Dead.

These traditions are neither perfectly homogeneous nor altogether discrete. In the biblical tradition, for example, there are significant differences between the Hebrew and Greek versions. In fact, in the Early Middle Ages the biblical tradition splits: the Hebrew Job, translated in the Vulgate, becomes the canonical version in medieval Europe, while the Septuagint Job provides authority for many of the apocryphal elaborations which proliferate. In the biblical tradition Job is sometimes impatient and rebellious. In the apocryphal tradition Job is always pious and patient, just as he is in the ecclesiastical tradition. And in the ecclesiastical tradition certain nearly blasphemous verses from the Book of Job are turned to devotional use, while the entire Book of Job becomes the basis for exegetical reflections on Christian doctrine.

More often a work will be indebted primarily to one of the

traditions, even though in a few places it may draw on one or both of the others. The history of Job in medieval art shows this very clearly. Yet, art historians have overlooked this tripartite typology of the iconography of Job, although individual representations of the Job legend have been studied in great detail.[3] They have not noticed that we can group works according to whether their primary indebtedness is to biblical, apocryphal, or ecclesiastical tradition. Consider scenes of Job and his wife. There are many scores of illustrations showing Job seated on a mound of ashes or a dungheap—it is usually impossible to say which—with his wife standing opposite, and both Job and his wife hold open scrolls on which are inscribed words from Job 2:9-10. There are also numerous illustrations of Job seated on an ashpile or dungheap, his wife opposite him extending bread in a cleft stick, on a palette, or sometimes on a spoon, while she covers her nose and mouth with a fold of her robe. Finally, Job is often portrayed on his ashpile or dungheap, flanked by his wife and Satan, who berate him and beat him, respectively, or we find scenes of the flagellation of Job by his wife and Satan paired with scenes of the Flagellation of Christ.

These three very different kinds of portraits of Job and his wife embody motifs from the biblical, apocryphal, and ecclesiastical traditions, respectively (see figs. 1, 2, 4; 7; 13). Their inconsistencies and incongruities, which we might mistake for medieval fancy running free, mainly reflect the various traditions of Job on which medieval artists drew. Similarly, in medieval literature Job was portrayed as a pious man complaining that God has done him wrong, an invincible stoic ready to take whatever he gets, a serene believer in the afterlife, or a prophet of Christ—or all of these at once. It was by combining these and other motifs from biblical, apocryphal, and ecclesiastical traditions that medieval writers made their unique contribution to the growth of the Job legend, capturing some of the grandeur and complexity of the biblical story even as they recast it almost beyond recognition.

1 | Biblical Origins

IN THE DEVELOPMENT of both the Jewish and Christian canons, the position of the Book of Job among the other books of the Bible tended to vary. Jewish tradition records at least three different orders for Job and the other poetical books in the "Writings" (Hebrew, Ketuvim; Greek, Hagiographa), the third division of the Old Testament, following the Pentateuch and Prophets. And among the Church Fathers there was considerable disagreement over whether Job would be more suitably placed among the poetical books, the histories, or after the Prophets. Since the Council of Trent, however, the order of biblical books favored by Jerome in the Vulgate—with Job following Esther and at the head of a poetic trilogy whose two other members are Psalms and Proverbs—has prevailed in the West.[1]

In addition to Job's place in the canon, the genre of Job has also presented something of a puzzle. According to some long-standing traditions, it has been considered an epic or a drama. But the consensus of modern scholarship is that Job is wisdom literature, a genre that includes Proverbs, Ecclesiastes, certain psalms, parts of Esther, and (among the Apocrypha) Ecclesiasticus, parts of the Book of Tobit, the Wisdom of Solomon, parts of 1 Esdras, 4 Maccabees, and parts of the Book of Baruch.[2] Wisdom writings usually take the form of a debate, a dialogue, or—as is most often the case in the Bible—a lengthy, didactic poetic monologue. But it is the subject matter rather than the form that is most characteristic of the genre. The wisdom books, as O. S. Rankin writes, "study particularly all the great human motives of conduct—gratitude, friendship, love, hate, wealth, reputation. Wisdom is the ability to assess truly the values of life. It is in the Wisdom literature where reflection is made upon the chief good . . . upon man in relation to the universe . . . upon the possibilities of religious faith over against the circumstances, facts, and experiences of life; upon the higher and lower nature of man . . . upon the problem of evil and the subject of divine providence" (p. 4). There is also a more worldly and practical side to the genre, reflected in cynically prudential apothegms like:

> Give a pledge for a stranger and know no peace;
> refuse to stand surety and be safe
>
> (Proverbs 11:15)

and in the more characteristically lofty:

> The kindly man will be blessed,
> for he shares his food with the poor.
>
> (Proverbs 22:9)

Wisdom writers also frequently reflect on natural wonders—wild beasts, the sea, and the heavenly bodies (for example, Ecclesiasticus 42:15-43:33; Job 38-41, and so on). The primary subject of their wonderment, however, is Wisdom itself, usually personified as a mysterious female figure and extolled in richly figurative language (Proverbs 9:1-6; Job 28; Ecclesiasticus 1:1-10, 6:18-22; Wisdom of Solomon 6:12ff, and so on). The wisdom books tend sometimes to be pessimistic, including passages of gloomy ruminations on human destiny that some scholars think may be a reflex of Greek or Egyptian influence on Israelite thought, as in these verses from Ecclesiastes:

> Again, I considered all the acts of oppression here under the sun; I saw the tears of the oppressed, and I saw that there was no one to comfort them . . . I counted the dead happy because they were dead, happier than the living who are still in life.
>
> (4:1-3)

or these verses from Job:

> Why should the sufferer be born to see the light?
> Why is life given to men who find it so bitter? /
> They wait for death but it does not come,
> They seek it more eagerly than hidden treasure.[3]
>
> (3:20-21)

One can hardly question the classification of the Book of Job as wisdom literature—its dialogue form, reflections on reward and punishment, praise of Wisdom, and catalogues of natural wonders are striking points of affinity with the other biblical wisdom books. Yet, as Marvin Pope remarks, Job contains a good deal of "anti-wisdom wisdom." One senses that to a large extent its raison d'être was to probe divine justice, not merely to assert it, and to question traditional wisdom, rather than merely to expound it. And so the essential validity of the classification of Job as wisdom literature should not keep us from going deeper in our understanding of its uniqueness; for it is the uniqueness of Job and its particular complexities that we must fathom if later we are to come to grips with the rich and varied literary and artistic lineage of which it is the progenitor.

A blameless, God-fearing, and extraordinarily prosperous man named Job lived in the land of Uz. One day God, addressing Satan in the heavenly assembly, pointed out Job as an example of perfect righteousness: "You will find no one like him on earth, a man of blameless and upright life, who fears God and sets his face against wrong-doing" (1:8). Satan replies that Job is God-fearing because he is prosperous, and that if he were to suffer material losses he would curse God. The Lord gives Satan power over all that Job has, only Job himself may not be touched. In one day, Job loses his shepherds, herdsmen, camel drivers, herds, flocks, and all his children, but still he does not "charge God with unreason" (1:22).

At the next heavenly assembly, the Lord challenges Satan with Job's constancy in adversity. Satan replies that physical adversity would cause Job to curse God, even if material losses had failed to upset his faith: "There is nothing the man will grudge to save himself" (2:5). When the Lord agrees to this further trial, Satan proceeds to smite Job "with running sores from head to foot" (2:8). And despite his wife's advice: "Curse God and die" (2:9), Job is as steadfast in his acceptance of misfortune as he was in his acceptance of prosperity.

Eliphaz, Bildad, and Zophar come from afar to condole with and comfort Job. Job curses the day of his birth and laments his unhappy fate at great length in a series of debates with his comforters touching on righteousness, sin, reward, and punishment. Job proclaims his innocence of sin while his comforters insist that he must have been guilty of grave sins to undergo such suffering (3:1-31:37). Then Elihu, a fourth comforter who appears as if from nowhere, rebukes the other comforters and offers an answer of his own to Job's plight. God then speaks to Job "out of the tempest" (38:1), rebukes but then vindicates him, and then forgives the three comforters "for not speaking of Him as they ought," but only after Job has prayed for them. Neither Elihu nor Satan is mentioned again.

Job is restored to even greater prosperity than he enjoyed before his trial. Another ten children are born to him, and he dies "at a very great age" (42:17).

Of course when we *read* the Book of Job, the inadequacies of such a summary loom before us. Perhaps its most readily apparent flaw is that it distorts the true proportions of the work: the poetic dialogues involving Job, his comforters, and the Lord (3-42:7) take up more than nine-tenths of the book. Furthermore, the summary conceals the fact that chapters 1-2 and 42:7-17 constitute a prose frame for chapters 3-42:6, the poetic core of the work.[4] This structural division is by no means negligible, for, along with certain linguistic and narrative evidence, it has led many scholars to hypothesize the prior existence of a prose folktale of Job adapted by the author of the poetic dialogues as prologue and epilogue to his own composition.[5] Other evidence in favor of this theory is that the prologue and epilogue to the Book of Job have the structural simplicity and independent coherence that we would expect to find in a very ancient folktale. In addition, there are discrepancies between the events of the epilogue and the apparent thematic thrust of the dialogues, and some readers take these discrepancies to be further evidence of the faulty melding of originally independent compositions.

Other questions that the summary raises, and that the Book of Job itself leaves unanswered, are of even greater immediacy. Who was Job? Was he an Israelite? Where is the land of Uz? Are there any historical connections between this righteous man and other righteous men in the Old Testament?[6] That the desire to answer these questions arose early in the history of the Job legend is evident from the many post-biblical attempts to endow Job with a local habitation and a more familiar name, complete with genealogy. For example, in the version of the Book of Job in the Greek Bible (Septuagint) we find the following concluding passage not found in the Hebrew:

> It is written, however, that he [Job] will rise again with those whom the Lord raises up. This [man] is explained from the Syriac Book as living in the land of Ausis, on the borders of Edom and Arabia; formerly his name was Jobab. He took an Arabian wife and sired a son whose name was Ennon. But he himself was the son of his father Zare[th], one of the sons of Esau, and of his mother Bosorra, so that he was the fifth from Abraham. Now these were the kings that reigned in Edom, over which land he also ruled: first Balak, the son of Beor, and the name of his city was Dennaba; and after Balak, Jobab who is called Job . . . [formerly his name was Jobab, but his father was Zareth from the rising of the sun.][7]

In the pseudepigraphal *Testament of Job*—and in Aramaic, Coptic, Arabic, and Hebrew legends as well—there are attempts similar to this one in the Septuagint to rationalize the biblical Job's apparent ahistoricity, attempts to flesh out a narrative that is at once economical to the point of obscurity in its presentation of foreground detail yet at the same time seems "fraught with background."[8]

In the first chapter of the Book of Job we meet *hasatan*, "the satan," or literally, "the adversary," a shadowy figure in the heavenly assembly who is allowed to propose a wager with the Lord that entails the otherwise unmotivated suffering of His blameless and most perfect servant. What sort of theology will account for this scene and its portrayal of God's capricious behavior? If we think of a traditionally "patient Job," then what shall we make of Job's lament: "Have I the strength to wait? What end have I to expect, that I should be patient?" (6:11), or his other impatient outbursts in the poem?

Still other questions arise: Why does Satan disappear from the story after the opening scenes in heaven?[9] Can we distinguish the three comforters' arguments or do they all merely repeat one another?[10] Why are the comforters chastised by the Lord when all along they have been arguing His case? Are Elihu's speeches an integral part of the work or are they later interpolations?[11] Is the last cycle of speeches in need of rearrangement?[12] What does chapter 28, the "wisdom poem," have to do with the rest of the book?[13] What is the genre of the work? Though we may accept its primary classification as wisdom literature, may we not still wonder to what extent it has affinities with epic, drama, or some mixed form?[14] When was the Book of Job written? Was it originally written in Hebrew? Or is the version we have a translation?[15] Perhaps most important of all are thematic questions: Why did Job suffer, and what was his consolation? What relevance could this consolation have for men reading the Book of Job as a divinely inspired tale?

These questions have furnished subject matter for many articles and books; I do not expect to answer them all definitively in a chapter. Bishop Lowth's opening remark in his Oxford University lecture on Job is even more pertinent today than it was over two hundred years ago: "Such a diversity of opinions has prevailed in the learned world concerning the nature and design of the Poem of Job, that the only point in which commentators seem to agree, is the extreme obscurity of the subject" (p. 176).

Fortunately, some of the most obscure issues surrounding the poem—the question of interpolations, jumbled passages, and rescension by emendation—are for our purposes of little importance. It is fairly safe to say that those transmutations of Job in Western literature and art which do not rely entirely on the apocryphal or ecclesiastical traditions derive from the biblical tradition preserved in the Masoretic Bible, the Septuagint, the Vulgate, and their immediate descendants, and not from some hypothetical *ur*-text. The meaning and coherence of the *extant* biblical versions of the Job legend are thus essential preliminary topics in a study of the later history of the theme in literature and art. Textual studies of the Book of Job are extremely valuable for what they can teach us about the poem in its original state, for the obscure phrases or allusions on which they may shed light, but they are of much less significance for an historical study of Job as a theme and an idea. As Northrop Frye has said of the Book of Job: "Guesswork about what the poem may originally have been or meant is useless, as it is only the version we know that has had any influence on our literature."[16] Furthermore, as we have learned from the recent discovery of an Aramaic paraphrase (*targum*) of Job in the caves of Qumran, the biblical story has circulated in its present putatively jumbled form since at least the second century B.C.[17]

By assuming the internal consistency and coherence of the text of the Book of Job—admittedly a vexed but, as we now know, a very ancient assumption—we adopt the point of view of virtually every pre-twentieth-century writer and artist who has portrayed Job. Even those medieval authors and artists who seem to know the Job legend primarily through an intervening work—for example, the *Testament of Job* or Gregory the Great's *Moralia*—are very likely to know the biblical story as well, and on occasion advert to it. To appreciate both the degree and the significance of an author's divergence from or adherence to the biblical tradition, we need first to understand the Book of Job. What did the author of the Book of Job intend to say about the purpose and outcome of Job's righteous suffering? What is supposed to be the general relevance or exemplary force of his story?

Many scholars think that the biblical portrayal of Job's unearned misery was intended to discredit, or at least to call into question, older biblical teachings on the subject of reward and punishment.[18] What these teachings entailed is well encapsulated by O. S. Rankin, who explains that "the simple and thorough-going theory that righteousness brings to individuals and to people material reward, and that evil brings material loss and penalty . . . may be termed for the sake of convenience the Deuteronomist theory, since it is applied to Israel's history, as consistently as seemed possible by the Deuteronomist redactors of Israel's historical records, as a religious interpretative principle, and is elaborately worked out in the twenty-eighth chapter of the Book of Deuteronomy itself (cf. Lev. 26)" (p. 77).

Now the precise language in Deuteronomy is worth quoting at some length, for there are striking points of contact between the following passages and the opening chapters of Job:

> If you will obey the Lord your God by diligently observing all his commandments which I lay upon you this day, then the Lord your God will raise you high above all nations of the earth, and all these blessings shall come to you and light upon you, because you obey the Lord your God.
>
> (Deut. 28:1-2)

> But if you do not obey the Lord your God by diligently observing all his commandments and statutes which I lay upon you this day, then all these maledictions shall come to you and light upon you.
>
> (28:15)

> May the Lord strike you with Egyptian boils and with tumours, scabs, and itches, for which you will find no cure. May the Lord strike you with madness, blindness, and bewilderment; so that you will grope about in broad daylight just as a blind man gropes in darkness, and will fail to find your way. You will also be oppressed and robbed, day in, day out, with no one to save you.
>
> (28:27-29)

> Your sons and daughters will be given to another people while you look on; your eyes will strain after them all day long, and you will be powerless . . . May the Lord strike you on knee and leg with malignant boils for which you will find no cure; they will spread from the sole of your foot to the crown of your head.
>
> (28:32-35)

Although these passages are addressed to the Israelites as a nation, it is easy to see how they came to be applied to individual destinies. If we keep in mind their unquestionable orthodoxy and recall at the same time the destruction and robbery of Job's cattle, the loss of his children, and his "running sores from head to foot" (Job 2:8), it is easy to see how Job's comforters, reasoning *post hoc propter hoc*, assumed that he was being punished for some wrongdoing.[19] Although we may find their tone unfeeling and their religious hectoring offensive, there is no denying that their words show them to be faithful proponents of the traditional Deuteronomist ethical teaching.

Eliphaz:

> For consider, what innocent man has ever perished?
> Where have you seen the upright destroyed? /
> This I know, that those who plough mischief and sow trouble /
> reap as they have sown; /
> they perish at the blast of God
> and are shrivelled by the breath of his nostrils.
>
> (4:7-9)

Bildad:

> Does God pervert judgment?
> Does the Almighty pervert justice? /
> Your sons sinned against him,
> so he left them to be victims of their own iniquity . . .
> if you are innocent and upright,
> then indeed will he watch over you . . .
> Be sure, God will not spurn the blameless man,
> nor will he grasp the hand of the wrongdoer.
>
> (8:3-4, 6, 20)

Zophar:

> Surely you know that this has been so since time began,
> since man was first set on the earth: /
> the triumph of the wicked is short lived,
> the glee of the godless lasts but a moment? . . .
> God vents his anger upon him
> and rains on him cruel blows.
>
> (20:4-5, 23)

To these passages we may add the similar testimony of Elihu:

> But listen to me, you men of good sense.
> Far be it from God to do evil
> or the Almighty to play false! /

> For he pays a man according to his work
> and sees that he gets what his conduct deserves. /
> The truth is, God does no wrong,
> the Almighty does not pervert justice.
>
> (34:10-12)

Ignoring for the moment possible differences in tone and emphasis in the comforters' speeches, it is clear from the preceding passages that they are unanimous in their assent to the Deuteronomist theory of justice.[20] But Job's views are for the most part in sharp contrast to theirs. He argues that God dispenses reward and punishment in a capricious, even draconian way:

> But it is all one; therefore I say,
> 'He destroys blameless and wicked alike.' /
> When a sudden flood brings death,
> he mocks the plight of the innocent. /
> The land is given over to the power of the wicked,
> and the eyes of its judges are blindfold.
>
> (9:22-24)

> Why do the wicked enjoy long life,
> hale in old age, and great and powerful? /
> They live to see their children settled,
> their kinsfolk and descendants flourishing; /
> their families are secure and safe;
> the rod of God's justice does not reach them.
>
> (21:7-9)

The juxtaposition of all these speeches reveals a thematic crux in the poem: Is there a direct correspondence between a man's conduct and his fate? Except for one startling reversal which we shall consider below, Job is sure that there is not, while his comforters are sure that there is. When the Lord speaks from the tempest the debate is squelched. He says to Eliphaz: "I am angry with you and your two friends, because you have not spoken as you ought about me, as my servant Job has done" (42:7).

Thus the doctrine of exact retribution appears to have been refuted on at least two counts: the Lord rebuffs the three comforters who upheld it and vindicates Job who attacked it;

and, as we witness in the prologue, suffering may come as a result of a wager between God and Satan and not as a punishment for sin. As for Elihu, whose words the Lord neither condemns nor praises, we are simply left wondering.

But is all this really the case?

We begin to suspect otherwise more than halfway through the poem when, in chapter 27, Job reverses himself and upholds the Deuteronomist theory:

> I will teach you what is in God's power,
> I will not conceal the purpose of the Almighty. /
> If all of you have seen these things,
> why then do you talk such empty nonsense? /
> This is the lot prescribed by God for the wicked,
> and the ruthless man's reward from the Almighty. /
> He may have many sons, but they will fall by the sword,
> and his offspring will go hungry; /
> the survivors will be brought to the grave by pestilence,
> and no widows will weep for them. /
> He may heap up silver like dirt
> and get himself piles of clothes; /
> he may get them, but the righteous will wear them,
> and his silver will be shared among the innocent.
>
> (27:11-17)

And our suspicions are strengthened by the prose epilogue to the poem, chapter 42:7-17, in which the author dwells on the temporal side of Job's restoration, itemizing with apparent relish Job's material wealth, children, descendants, and longevity. In these instances, Job and the Job-poet both appear to have repudiated the view that no connection exists between a man's righteousness and his material reward.

To answer the apparent contradiction, many scholars would assert that Job's speech in chapter 27 must be reassigned to Zophar and the evidence of the epilogue ignored, for it was not written by the poet of the dialogues—so the argument goes—and therefore it does not pose any real contradiction.[21] Marvin Pope's view is somewhat less extreme. He writes: "The fact that the Epilogue upholds the discredited doctrine of exact retribution . . . was doubtless a feature of the ancient folk tale that could not be altered. It is hard to imagine how else the story could end. It would scarcely do to leave Job in his misery after he had been vindicated. Perhaps the most significant line in the Epilogue is xlii.10 which seems to put Job's restoration in a temporal and perhaps causal nexus with his intercessory prayer for his friends."[22]

The remark about Job's intercessory prayer for his friends is worth pausing over, but more for what it implies about the structure of the poem than for what it says about the terms of Job's restoration. For Pope fails to notice that by juxtaposing this closing scene of Job praying for his friends with the opening scene of Job praying for his children (1:5), we discover that the completeness of Job's restoration has been reinforced by a careful symmetry in the narrative. But we must reject as highly improbable Pope's tentatively offered suggestion that Job is restored only after, and because, he interceded for his friends. It implies that Job was lacking in some way, whereas the Lord Himself says that Job was "a man of blameless and upright life, who fears God and sets his face against wrongdoing" (1:8). Any attempt to find Job's flaw, to accuse him of pride or overrighteousness, or to make his restoration contingent upon intercessory prayers for his friends is in principle misdirected—as misdirected as were the attacks of his would-be comforters.[23]

Rankin, on the other hand, has argued that the Book of Job was in no way meant to discredit the doctrine of exact retribution in the first place, and so the epilogue poses no impossible contradictions:

> It is true that in his criticism of the divine justice Job brings forward instances where flagrant wickedness remains unpunished (21), but this brings us no farther than do the complaints or reflections upon prosperity of the wicked made by upholders of the orthodox creed (cf. Jer.12.1-6; Ps. 37, 49, etc.). When Job invokes just retribution and God's wrath upon his defamers with the warning, "Fear ye the sword!" (19.29) we perceive that he does not discard the familiar doctrine . . . The traditional doctrine of reward and retribution does receive dismissal within the Old Testament, but this is in a writing (Ecclesiastes, Qoheleth) which is characteristically unrepresentative of Old Testament piety.
>
> The effect of the Divine Speeches in their dropping of the categories of reward and retribution is to separate the problem of

> theodicy from these categories. But in consequence we are left with faith and not with a refinement of the idea of reward, and it would be reading too much into the Divine Speeches if we were to conclude that the author desired to deny current Deuteronomist theory of God's retributive justice (cf. 38.12f.).
>
> (pp. 90-91, 93)

Even if one does not fully agree with Rankin's extreme position—for there is no denying that God vindicates Job and that Job impugned the Deuteronomist theory—to think of the Book of Job as a straightforward attempt to revise obsolete Deuteronomist dogma is clearly to oversimplify. If we accept the proposition that Job discredits the Deuteronomist theory, then we must ask ourselves what theory the poem offers in its stead? And if the author of Job did not wish to discredit the Deuteronomist theory, is there any way to explain Job's undeserved suffering?

The answer, I believe, lies in the poet's complex and sometimes paradoxical presentation of a multiplicity of answers to the problem of righteous suffering.[24] And, to be sure, one of these answers is a modified version of the Deuteronomist theory:[25] The epilogue stresses Job's material well-being after his vindication to preclude converse, inverse, or obverse conclusions about the Deuteronomist theory; to preclude, for example, the conclusion that a suffering man is necessarily righteous or that a prosperous and happy man is necessarily sinful. This leaves the reader with a theory of reward and retribution asserting, in essence, that if the distribution of happiness and prosperity is not always just, neither is it always unjust—a theory admittedly much diluted, but not altogether discredited.

One final bit of evidence regarding the thematic propriety of the epilogue is found in Job's peroration (chapter 29), an unequivocal appeal for temporal restoration:

> If I could only go back to the old days,
> to the time when God was watching over me, /
> when his lamp shone above my head,
> and by its light I walked through the darkness! /
> If I could be as in the days of my prime,
> when God protected my home, /
> while the Almighty was still there at my side,

and my servants stood round me, /
while my path flowed with milk,
and the rocks streamed oil!

(29:2-6)

The epilogue, chapter 42:7-17, in which Job receives what he pleads for in chapter 29, is not, as Pope and others seem to think, merely a concession to the exigencies of an unwieldy plot; nor is it an inartistic compromise necessitated by the poet's failure of imagination when faced with the task of bringing his story to a satisfying conclusion. If the epilogue seems to confute the evidence in the rest of the Book of Job on the question of the Deuteronomist theory, then perhaps that is because it is meant to do so. In one sense, the restoration of Job's family and his material wealth is another aspect of his vindication.

By a "multiplicity of answers" I am not suggesting that the Book of Job bristles with the tensions and ambiguities that critics find in most literary texts (though these may not be entirely irrelevant in the present case). What I mean instead is something very straightforward: the Job-poet offers several, and in some instances contradictory, answers to one question, Why do good men suffer?

Now, for most of us, the suggestion that six or seven individually insufficient or contradictory answers to a single profound question can be cumulatively more valid than each answer would be on its own is at best extremely doubtful. Yet the presentation of a multiplicity of not necessarily consistent answers to a single profound question was a common occurrence in Ancient Near Eastern theology. As Henri Frankfort writes: "The ancients did not attempt to solve the ultimate problems confronting man by a single and coherent theory: that has been the method of approach since the time of the Greeks. Ancient thought—mythopoeic, 'myth-making' thought—admitted side by side certain *limited* insights, which were held to be *simultaneously* valid, each in its proper context, each corresponding to a definite avenue of approach."[26] We do not have to invoke recent critical theories of ambiguity or polysemous narration to account for our discovery in Job of this philosophical strategy.

One answer to the question of righteous suffering that the Book of Job strongly implies is that the righteous do not always suffer—up to the time we meet him, Job has had a life full of prosperity; and even when they do suffer, their suffering may last only for a short time and, like Job, they may subsequently be restored to well-being. This of course is a problematic if not altogether a trivial answer to the theodicy problem, but it is an element in the thematic matrix of the Book of Job of which many later adapters of the Job legend take note.

Another answer to righteous suffering in Job is implicit in the prologue, chapters 1:6-12 and 2:1-8. God, as we learn by eavesdropping on the heavenly assembly, allows Job's suffering because it is dictated by the terms of a wager He has entered into at the instigation of Satan. This shifts the question of injustice on earth to a heavenly arena and makes it a matter of divine caprice if not outright weakness; nevertheless, it does allow the reader to conceive of injustice as a purposeful if enigmatic feature of creation. To medieval readers, the idea that Job's righteous suffering vindicated him before God and defeated Satan was very appealing. As the second-century Greek theologian Clement of Alexandria observed: "[Job] it was who overcame the tempter by patience, and at once testified and was testified to by God."[27] But from Job's point of view, was there a victory, and if so, over whom? Although the reader may be aware of the miraculous heavenly effects of Job's steadfast suffering, Job himself never learns that he has helped the Lord to win a wager.

A third answer to righteous suffering in Job is the explicit and repeated valuation of suffering as a pedagogical or purgative experience. Eliphaz asserts the salutary nature of suffering in his first discourse, when he addresses Job in these words: "Happy the man whom God rebukes! Therefore do not reject the discipline of the Almighty" (5:17).[28] And some commentators think that this view of Job's suffering is Elihu's major contribution to the debate, since we find it in the following intensely figurative passage:

> In dreams, in visions of the night,
> when deepest sleep falls upon men, /

while they sleep on their beds, God makes them listen,
and his correction strikes them with terror. /
To turn a man from reckless conduct,
to check the pride of mortal man, /
at the edge of the pit he holds him back alive
and stops him from crossing the river of death.

(33:15-18)

And again, if less poetically, in the following verse: "Those who suffer he rescues through suffering and teaches them by the discipline of affliction" (36:15). Even Job, at least in the following verse, seems to acknowledge that suffering is a divinely ordained test: "But he knows me in action or at rest; when he tests me, I prove to be gold" (23:10).

Here we notice something very curious indeed. Together with his antagonistic interlocutors, Eliphaz and Elihu, Job seems to assert the pedagogic or purgative effects of suffering, whereas elsewhere in the poem he vehemently denies that his suffering has any purpose whatsoever. This reversal on Job's part, along with the similar one in chapter 27:11-23 when he defends the Deuteronomist theory, are just two instances of a general proleptic movement in the poem and of a rhythm of repetition and parallelism that is a key to its theme and narrative structure. The poem affords other instances of this stylistic device—Job's intercessory prayer for his friends in the last chapter, for example, which parallels his sacrifices and prayers for his children in the first chapter—yet I know of not a single study of the Book of Job in which the full extent of its significance has been appreciated. On the contrary, it is usually imbalance and lack of parallelism in the narrative that critics have stressed: for example, that Satan does not reappear in the epilogue, that Zophar does not speak a third time, or that Elihu's speeches go unanswered.[29]

The passages juxtaposed below point up a striking anticipation of an important motif in Job, the Leviathan-sea-monster motif, and they illustrate further the vital role that prolepsis and repetition play in the overall style and meaning of the poem.

From Job's speeches:

> Perish the day when I was born
> and the night which said, 'A man is conceived'! /
> . . . Cursed be it by those whose magic binds even
> the monster of the deep,
> who are ready to tame Leviathan himself with spells.
>
> (3:3, 8)

> Am I the monster of the deep, am I the sea-serpent,
> that thou settest a watch over me?
>
> (7:12)

From the Lord's speeches:

> Can you pull out the Leviathan[30] with a gaff?
> or can you slip a noose round its tongue? / . . .
> Will it plead with you for mercy
> or beg its life with soft words? /
> Will it enter into an agreement with you
> to become your slave for life?
>
> (41:1, 3-4)

Read synoptically, these passages reveal that the Lord's oft-quoted words about Leviathan—words, incidentally, that many scholars regard as interpolations or at best non-sequiturs[31]—are in fact anticipated and perhaps even to some extent motivated by Job's words earlier in the poem. As we learn from 3:8 and 7:12 (see also 9:13 and 26:12-13), Job respects the power of the Leviathan and those whose "magic" binds it; the Lord's rhetorical question about the power of the Leviathan therefore comes as a direct, ironic response to Job's rhetorical question and apostrophe on the same subject. One scholar has aptly described the Lord's debating technique in this passage and elsewhere in the divine speeches as "education through overwhelming."[32] It is well worth noticing, however, that in vaunting the great discrepancy between the power of man and the power of Leviathan, the Lord has taken his cue from Job.

Other thematically significant prolepses in the poem are highlighted in the following passages.

Eliphaz:

A word stole into my ears,
and they caught the whisper of it; /
in the anxious visions of the night,
when a man sinks into deepest sleep, /
terror seized me and shuddering;
the trembling of my body frightened me. /
A wind brushed my face
and made the hairs bristle on my flesh; /
and a figure stood there whose shape I could not discern,
an apparition loomed before me,
and I heard the sound of a low voice: /
'Can mortal man be more righteous than God,
or the creature purer than his Maker? /
If God mistrusts his own servants
and finds his messengers at fault, /
how much more those that dwell in houses whose walls are clay,
whose foundations are dust,
which can be crushed like a bird's nest /
or torn down between dawn and dark,
how much more shall such men perish outright and unheeded, /
die, without ever finding wisdom?'

(4:12-21)

Bildad:

Authority and awe rest with him
who has established peace in his realm on high. /
His squadrons are without number;
at whom will they not spring from ambush? /
How then can a man be justified in God's sight,
or one born of woman be innocent? /
If the circling moon is found wanting,
and the stars are not innocent in his eyes, /
much more so man who is but a maggot,
mortal man who is only a worm.

(25:2-6)

Zophar:

Can you fathom the mystery of God,
can you fathom the perfection of the Almighty? /

It is higher than heaven; you can do nothing.
It is deeper than Sheol; you can know nothing.

(11:7-8)

Elihu:

Well, this is my answer: You are wrong.
God is greater than man; /
why then plead your case with him?
for no one can answer his arguments. /
Indeed, once God has spoken
he does not speak a second time to confirm it. /
In dreams, in visions of the night,
when deepest sleep falls upon men, /
while they sleep on their beds, God makes them listen,
and his correction strikes them with terror.

(33:12-16)

Job:

If I summoned him to court and he responded, /
I do not believe that he would listen to my plea— /
for he bears hard upon me for a trifle
and rains blows on me without cause; /
. . . If the appeal is to force, see how strong he is;
if to justice, who can compel him to give me a hearing?

(9:16-17, 19)

The Lord:

Then the Lord answered Job out of the tempest: /
Who is this whose ignorant words
cloud my design in darkness? /
Brace yourself and stand up like a man;
I will ask questions, and you shall answer. /
Where were you when I laid the earth's foundations?
Tell me, if you know and understand.

(38:1-4)

As these passages show, the idea of man's powerlessness in the face of the Lord's omnipotence is common currency in Job. It appears most prominently as the burden of the Lord's speeches, but it is anticipated in speeches by the three comforters, Elihu, and Job himself.

Even more arresting, primarily because it is usually overlooked, is Eliphaz's account of a dream vision that bears a striking resemblance to the theophany that Job experiences in chapters 38-41: Eliphaz feels a wind and hears a low voice that poses rhetorical questions that assert man's ignorance and insignificance; Job hears the Lord's voice out of the tempest and is asked similar rhetorical questions. This prolepsis is reinforced when the theophany motif is again adumbrated in Elihu's speech (33:15-16). But the central importance of the theophany motif is most firmly and definitively established by the cumulative anticipatory effect of Job's own words in a number of passages throughout the poem:

> But for my part I would speak with the Almighty
> and am ready to argue with God.
>
> (13:3)

> If he would slay me, I should not hesitate;
> I should still argue my cause to his face. /
> This at least assures my success,
> that no godless man may appear before him.
>
> (13:15-16)

> Grant me these two conditions only,
> and then I will not hide myself out of thy sight: /
> take thy heavy hand clean away from me
> and let not the fear of thee strike me with dread. /
> Then summon me, and I will answer;
> or I will speak first, and do thou answer me.
>
> (13:20-22)

> If only I knew how to find him,
> how to enter his court, /
> I would state my case before him
> and set out my arguments in full; /
> then I should learn what answer he would give
> and find out what he had to say.
>
> (23:3-5)

> Let me but call a witness in my defence!
> Let the Almighty state his case against me!
>
> (31:35)

When the long-awaited, oft-requested theophany finally takes place, it entails a rebuke of Job's presumption coupled with a magisterial catalogue of natural wonders, followed by Job's vindication and a rebuff to the comforters. Repeated anticipations of these motifs earlier in the poem are hard to overlook. In almost every speech, the comforters and Elihu had rebuked Job for his presumption and drawn his attention to the wonders of nature; and Job himself had all along expressed his awe at the manifestations of God's might in nature, once even quoting verbatim the words of Eliphaz to make the point ("oseh gedolot ve'en ḥeker, nifla'ot ad en mispar," "[The Lord] does great and unsearchable things, marvels without number," 5:9 and 9:10).[33]

What large thematic purpose does prolepsis in the Book of Job serve? The answer, it seems to me, is that by numerous anticipations throughout the poem of the Lord's arguments in the theophany, the Job-poet has allowed the fact of the theophany itself rather than its content to give a final shape to the poem and determine its meaning. The principal irony of the divine speeches is that by repeating what in essence has already been said earlier in the poem (excepting, of course, the comforters' charge that Job was suffering because he had sinned), they do not offer Job any more cogent explanation of his cruel fate than he has already heard.

Critics have recognized that Job does not find the answer to his questions "in a reasoned explanation or a theology, but in a religious experience . . . a firsthand experience of God."[34] What they have failed to appreciate fully, however, are the major stylistic devices by means of which the author of Job has so masterfully underlined this experience. It is through prolepsis and repetition that the stark and simple action of the Book of Job—especially its climactic action, the theophany—is allowed to overshadow its cognitive content. Job's last words in the poetic dialogue eloquently and concisely express the nonrational significance of the theophany:

> I know that thou canst do all things
> and that no purpose is beyond thee. /
> . . . I knew of thee then only by report,
> but now I see thee with my own eyes. /
> Therefore I melt away;
> I repent in dust and ashes.
>
> (42:2, 5-6)

Suddenly the issues debated in the dialogue are irrelevant. Seeing has brought to a halt all attempts to speak, to understand, or to know.

A fourth answer to Job's righteous suffering, then, is the poetic segment of the theophany (chapters 38-41), which may in and of itself be regarded as a part of Job's reward for steadfast suffering. It is not every righteous sufferer who is privileged to be browbeaten by the Lord in a personal confrontation.

Furthermore, in the segment of the theophany which continues into the prose epilogue, there is yet another element of Job's consolation, namely, the vindication of his rebelliousness. Although the Lord begins his remarks in the theophany by accusing Job of "ignorant words" (38:2), he ends up chiding Eliphaz and his two friends and praising Job (42:7), apparently for maintaining his innocence and for asserting in the face of the comforters' unrelenting, pietistic hectoring that, in his own case if not always in others, the Lord's administration of reward and retribution was capricious.[35] Though the Lord's response to Job remains ambiguous, in His rebuke of the comforters there is no ambiguity. The outcome is exactly as Job predicted in an earlier proleptic passage addressed to the comforters:

> Is it on God's behalf that you speak so wickedly,
> or in his defence that you allege what is false? /
> Must you take God's part,
> or put his case for him? /
> Will all be well when he examines you?
> Will you quibble with him as you quibble with a man? /
> He will most surely expose you
> if you take his part by falsely accusing me. /
> Will not God's majesty strike you with dread,

and terror of him overwhelm you? /
Your pompous talk is dust and ashes,
your defences will crumble like clay.

(13:7-12)

The vindication of Job's rebelliousness is a theme of the biblical Job legend that was, with very few exceptions, ignored in the Middle Ages. It was only in the nineteenth and twentieth centuries that critics came to see it as central to any interpretation of the legend. The nineteenth-century essayist, James Anthony Froude, for example, vindicated Job and condemned his comforters for their religious doctrine, not for their cruelty: "The self-constituted pleaders for Him, the acceptors of His person, were all wrong; and Job—the passionate, vehement, scornful, misbelieving Job—he had spoken the truth; he at least had spoken facts, and they had been defending a transient theory as an everlasting truth."[36] For readers in the Middle Ages, it would have been quite out of the question to describe Job and his comforters in these terms.

In the Middle Ages, on the other hand, Job's faith in a personal redeemer and his belief in an afterlife in which all of this world's injustices will be righted were considered to be his primary response to righteous suffering—even though the presence of these motifs in the biblical text is dubious at best. True, almost any verse in the Book of Job will yield the desired affirmation of life after death if the interpreter is ingenious enough. St. Ambrose, for example, found evidence of Job's faith in the afterlife in Job 3:3, which begins "Perish the day when I was born," on which he comments: "Job had recognized that to be born is the beginning of all woes, and therefore wishes that the day on which he was born might perish, so that the origin of all the troubles might be removed, and wished that the day of his birth might perish that he might receive the day of resurrection."[37] But the locus classicus for the view that Job believed both in a personal redeemer and in an afterlife is chapter 19:25-27. These are among the best known verses in the entire poem, yet as the following widely differing translations indicate, they are also among the most obscure:

Vulgate:

> Scio enim quod Redemptor meus vivit,
> Et in novissimo die de terra surrecturus sum; /
> Et rursum circumdabor pella mea,
> Et in carne mea videbo Deum meum. /
> Quem visurus sum ego ipse,
> Et oculi mei conspecturi sunt, et non alius;
> Reposita est haec spes mea in sinu meo.
>
> [For I know that my Redeemer liveth,
> and in the last day I shall rise out of the earth. /
> And I shall be clothed again with my skin,
> and in my flesh I shall see my God. /
> Whom I myself shall see,
> and my eyes shall behold, and not another:
> this my hope is laid up in my bosom.]

King James:

> For I know *that* my redeemer liveth, and *that* he shall stand at the latter *day* upon the earth: /
> And *though* after my skin worms destroy this *body*, yet in my flesh shall I see God: /
> Whom I shall see for myself, and mine eyes shall behold, and not another; *though* my reins be consumed within me.

New English Bible:

> But in my heart I know that my vindicator lives
> and that he will rise last to speak in court; /
> and I shall discern my witness standing at my side
> and see my defending counsel, even God himself, /
> whom I shall see with my own eyes,
> I myself and no other.

The progression from Vulgate to King James to New English Bible, with Job's faith in resurrection clear and incontestable in the first instance, cloudy in the second, and nonexistent in the third, is strikingly evident.

Part of the reason for the disparities between the translations is the difficulty of the Hebrew text, which contains several philological cruxes that no translation can entirely resolve.[38] Yet there can be little doubt that of the three translations cited it is the Vulgate version which founders and sinks most summarily on the shoals of the Hebrew original. Nevertheless, it is well worth pausing over, for it was usually the Vulgate that Western Church Fathers like Augustine, Gregory, and their followers had before them when they took Job 19:25-27 to signify Job's faith in resurrection and his hope for redemption through Christ.[39] The interpretation of these verses as a doxological pronouncement of faith in the resurrection of the dead and in redemption through Christ was to become a dominant theme in medieval literary and artistic representations of Job.

In the King James translation of 19:25-27 there is similar though slightly more ambiguous evidence of Job's faith in an afterlife and in a redeemer. I cite this version of Job 19:25-27 not because it contributes to our understanding of the original text but because it appears at the opening of the English burial service and is the version of this passage most often quoted in the English-speaking world. In addition, these verses from the King James have been set to music by Schütz, Bach, Handel, and others.

In turning to the New English Bible translation, we may address the main question at hand: To what extent is a belief in an afterlife and in a personal redeemer an element of Job's consolation? It is the view of the majority of modern scholars, reflected in the New English Bible, that, whatever the remaining textual obscurities, Job 19:25-27 has little or nothing to do with resurrection or the afterlife. And as for the notion that Job here expresses his hope for an intercessor of some kind, most modern scholars agree that the New English Bible translators have brought us closer to the meaning of the original by translating the Hebrew *go'el* not as "redeemer" but as "vindicator." As Pope explains, this "vindicator" is the same intercessor Job prays for in 9:33: "If only there were one to arbitrate between us and impose his authority on us both," and again in 16:19, which begins: "For look! my witness is in heaven."[40]

Though we may agree with Pope's claim that in 14:13-15 and 19:25-27 Job "gropes toward the idea of an afterlife,"[41] we must remain mindful of the fact that elsewhere in the poem Job speaks emphatically of the finality of death (for example, 10:20-21, 14:7-10, 16:22, and 17:13-16). It seems more likely, therefore, that Job 19:25-27 contains a proleptic plea for vindication and theophany, and that these verses are similar to the ones cited earlier, in which Job asserts his innocence and looks ahead to the time when it will be proved. In any event, the murkiness of this entire issue will be well worth recalling later on, when we observe how frequently and confidently Job was portrayed in the Middle Ages as a confirmed believer in resurrection.

One last thread in the thematic fabric of the poem that calls for some comment is Job's request in two separate instances —it is each time more an anguished plea than a request—for a permanent record of his trial:

> O that my words might be inscribed,
> O that they might be engraved in an inscription, /
> cut with an iron tool and filled with lead
> to be a witness in hard rock!
>
> (19:23-24)

> . . . if my accuser had written out his indictment,
> I would not keep silence and remain indoors
> [this line is transposed from verse 34].
> No! I would flaunt it on my shoulder
> and wear it like a crown on my head.
>
> (31:35b-36)

Despite the textual problems, almost as thorny as in 19:25-27, I would suggest that in these two passages we have a kind of literary immortality motif—Job's powerful and proleptic plea for the biblical immortality of which the Book of Job assures him.[42] This is a theme in the poem about which the critics, with only rare exceptions, are silent.[43] Nevertheless, there are, I think, a sufficient number of self-conscious references in the Bible to the theme of literary (that is, biblical) immortality to lend at least some measure of plausibility to the discovery of its appearance here in Job.[44] To cite probably the most notable appearance of the theme in the Hebrew Bible: when Moses makes his dramatic appeal to God to forgive the Israelites for worshipping the golden calf, he offers up this audacious challenge: "If thou wilt forgive them, forgive. But if not, blot out my name, I pray, from thy book which thou hast written." And God, relenting, replies: "It is the man who has sinned against me that I will blot out from my book" (Exodus 32:32-33). This exchange should mitigate our doubts about the availability of the literary immortality motif in the thought-world of the Old Testament.

In any event, as the following citation of the Vulgate version of the verses in question shows, in the most influential medieval text of the Book of Job the theme of literary immortality is even more explicit than in the Hebrew:

> Quis mihi tribuat ut scribantur sermones mei?
> Quis mihi det ut exarentur in libro, /
> Stylo ferreo et plumbi lamina,
> Vel celte sculpantur in silice?
>
> (19:23-24)
>
> Quis mihi tribuat auditorem,
> Ut desiderium meum audiat Omnipotens,
> Et librum scribat ipse qui iudicat, /
> Ut in humero meo portem illum,
> Et circumdem illum quasi coronam mihi?
>
> (31:35-36)

> [Who will grant me that my words may be written?
> who will grant me that they may be marked down in a book? /
> With an iron pen and in a plate of lead,
> or else be graven with an instrument in flint-stone?
>
> Who would grant me a hearer,
> that the Almighty may hear my desire:
> and that he himself that judgeth would write a book. /
> That I may carry it on my shoulder,
> and put it about me as a crown?]

Though most medieval authors overlooked this theme, there were a few who turned it to good use.

The principal responses to righteous suffering in the Book of Job may be summarized as follows:

(1) A modified Deuteronomist theory. Job is virtuous, yet his fortunes fluctuate: he starts out prosperous and happy, becomes impoverished and wretched, but is finally restored to prosperity and happiness. Although the correspondence between virtue and reward and sin and punishment is inexact, at least in Job's case the balances wind up tilted in the right direction.
(2) Vindicatory suffering. Job's steadfastness vindicates God in his wager with Satan.
(3) Purgative or pedagogical suffering. God inflicts Job's suffering to check his pride and complacency, to educate and strengthen him.
(4) Theophany. God speaks to Job, confirms his righteousness and rebukes the comforters, and, arguing a fortiori from the incomprehensibility of natural wonders, places the question of righteous suffering beyond human understanding.
(5) Righteous rebelliousness. God vindicates Job's protest and rebukes His would-be defenders, the comforters.
(6) Hope in a vindicator and in an afterlife. Job expresses a hope that he will be vindicated by an intercessor or that a witness—perhaps, somewhat paradoxically, even God Himself—will plead his case. There is a very faint possiblility that Job hopes for this in an afterlife.
(7) Biblical immortality. Job pleads for a written record of his ordeal. The Book of Job itself is a part of Job's reward and vindication.

We may draw important distinctions between these motifs on the basis of their spheres of relevance or applicability—that is, on the basis of whether or not they transcend the world of the poem. Thus motifs one, two, three, five, and six all retain a great part of their validity outside the context of the poem, whereas four and seven are valid only within it, and for Job alone. A similar dichotomy applies to the paradigmatic nature of Job's role: although Job's righteousness before the onset of his suffering and his pertinacious searching for God in the midst of it are meant to be exemplary, these are elements in the story which, in the very perfection of their accomplishment, set Job's life apart from the normal spheres of human experience and thereby limit his exemplary force. Almost everything about Job is mythical in its proportions and idealized in its perfection: his wealth as well as his righteousness, his suffering as well as his vindication and restoration. These are all aspects of his story that transcend the normal bounds of human life and allow, or force, a reader to keep his distance. Although this distance closes the reader off from the richness of Job's experience, it also makes more bearable the account of his enormous physical and psychic suffering. Unlike the names of most other important biblical heroes, Job has never been a popular name in either Jewish or Christian circles.[45]

Along these lines we should recall that in the province of the poem Job never learns that his steadfast suffering vindicates God, nor, we assume, does he learn that his ordeal becomes the subject of a biblical book. These additional discrepancies between Job's experience and knowledge of events and ours create a situation of intense dramatic irony. On the one hand they further prevent our identification with Job; on the other hand, by limiting his scope, they tend to make him more human, so that despite the distance between Job and the reader the latter still feels, with Kierkegaard, that "everything about him is so human."[46]

Because the Book of Job seems to abide its own contradictions, there is probably no point in trying to resolve this or any other major thematic issue in the poem definitively. As Paul Humbert writes: "We must be sure to avoid disarticulating this highly original book in the name of some formal classical canon, and to take it instead as it is, with its disparities and with its strange and majestic form; at the same time we must not close our eyes to its carefully conceived architecture" (p. 151; my translation). The Book of Job is too elusive and too multifaceted to be taken in under one rubric. This is surely a major reason it has endured in our culture as a consolation and stay.

Biblical allusions to the Job legend outside of the Book of Job—odds and ends of the tradition—are surprisingly numerous. From puzzling brief references to Job in Ezekiel 14: 12-14 and 14:19-20, we know for certain that Job's name—alongside the names of Noah and Danel (*sic*)—was a by-word for righteousness and that his legend was widely known as early as the sixth century B.C. (though perhaps not in the form in which it is preserved in the Book of Job).[47] And when James, in his General Epistle, exhorts his audience to be "patient and stout-hearted" (James 5:7), he adduces the example of Job in a way that assumes the currency and wide diffusion of the legend: "You have all heard how Job stood firm, and you have seen how the Lord treated him in the end" (5:11). Even more significant than either of these fugitive allusions, however, are the overt references to Job and extended analogies to certain facets of the Job legend in the Vulgate version of the Book of Tobias, a biblical work that was exceedingly popular in the Middle Ages.

Tobias, a virtuous Hebrew exiled by the Assyrians and living in Nineveh, "daily went among all his kindred, and comforted them, and distributed to every one as he was able, out of his goods: / He fed the hungry, and gave clothes to the naked, and was careful to bury the dead, and they [*sic*] that were slain" (1:19-20). As the continuation of the story shows, scrupulous attention to burial of the dead was Tobias' outstanding virtue—so much so that folklorists regard his story as an instance of the so-called Grateful Dead motif. This is not something he has in common with Job, but in his giving of alms he begins to resemble the Job of the Hebrew poem (chapter 31) as well as the Job of *The Testament of Job*. Still more indicative of the similarities between Job and Tobias is the following passage:

> Now it happened one day, that being wearied with burying, he came to his house, and cast himself down by the wall and slept. / And as he was sleeping, hot dung out of a swallow's nest fell upon his eyes, and he was made blind. / Now this trial the Lord therefore permitted to happen to him, that an example might be given to posterity of his patience, as also of holy Job. / For whereas he had always feared God from his infancy, and kept his commandments, he repined not against God because the evil of blindness had befallen him. / But continued immoveable in the fear of God, giving thanks to God all the days of his life. / For as the kings insulted over holy Job: so his relations and kinsmen mocked at his life, saying: / Where is thy hope, for which thou gavest alms, and buriedst the dead? / But Tobias rebuked them, saying: speak not so: / For we are the children of saints, and look for that life which God will give to those that never

> change their faith from him. / Now Anna his wife went daily to weaving work, and she brought home what she could get for their living by the labour of her hands. / Whereby it came to pass, that she received a young kid, and brought it home: / And when her husband heard it bleating, he said: Take heed, lest perhaps it be stolen, restore ye it to its owners, for it is not lawful for us either to eat or to touch anything that cometh by theft. / At these words his wife being angry answered: It is evident thy hope is come to nothing, and thy alms now appear. / And with these and other such like words she upbraided him.
>
> (2:10-23)

The explicit allusions to Job's patience and to the comforters in Job as "kings" are difficult to explain with exclusive reference to the Hebrew Book of Job. Furthermore, in the resigned and pious speeches of Tobias under the lash of his righteous suffering, in the expanded role of his wife, and in the blasphemous questions of his would-be comforters, Tobias' story is also very similar to the story of Job—once again, however, not as we find it in the Hebrew poem, but as it is in the Septuagint and especially, in more fully developed form, in *The Testament of Job*.

Though it is likely that there are other allusions to Job in both the Old Testament Apocrypha and in the New Testament, none is nearly as significant for a study of the medieval Job legend as this one in the Book of Tobias.[48] Like the much less substantial allusions in Ezekiel and James, it points to the existence of a tradition collateral with and different from the one in the Hebrew Book of Job. Where did this other tradition come from? What were its points of contact with and divergence from the tradition preserved in the Hebrew poem? Initial answers to these questions are to be found in the Septuagint version of the Book of Job—a version similar to the one that the author of Tobias no doubt had in mind when he spoke of Job, and one that was to influence numerous later authors as well.

The origins of the Greek translation of the Hebrew Bible known as the Septuagint reach as far back as the second or perhaps even the third century B.C., to a time when the need arose among Alexandrian Jews for a uniform translation of the Old Testament into the Greek vernacular.[49] No translation of the Hebrew Bible was to rival the Septuagint and its several recensions in historical importance; its decisive role in the spread of Christianity is hard to overestimate. As Swete asserts, "The Christian Churches of Greek-speaking countries throughout the Empire read the Old Testament in the Alexandrian version"; moreover, Clement of Rome and Irenaeus of Lyons both knew the Old Testament in the Greek of the Septuagint—it was only the North African Church to which the Greek Bible was "a sealed book" (pp. 87-88).

The translators of the Septuagint made changes in both the plot and theology of the Book of Job that were to have far-reaching consequences for later traditions of Job.[50] Evaluating the methodology of the translation, Gehman writes, "In many instances, departures from a literal rendering can be ascribed to an exegesis which had a theological basis" (p. 231). One finds that the Greek translator consistently introduced changes designed to tone down Job's presumptuousness and eliminate his most impious remarks from the Hebrew. Perhaps fed by older Hebrew and possibly by other Near Eastern traditions, the Septuagint Job thus represents an early stage in what might be called "the other tradition" in the biblical history of Job. The following examples of changes introduced by the Greek translator are chosen from among the many adduced by Gehman (pp. 232-238):

Hebrew:

> While he was still speaking, another messenger arrived and said, 'God's fire flashed from heaven. It struck the sheep and the shepherds and burnt them up.'

Greek:

> Another messenger came, and said to Job: Fire hath fallen from heaven and burnt up the sheep.
>
> (1:16)

Hebrew:

> But it is all one; therefore I say,
> 'He destroys blameless and wicked alike.'

Greek:

> Say, then, wrath destroyeth
> the great and powerful.
>
> (9:22)

Hebrew:

> But for my part I would speak with the Almighty
> and am ready to argue with God.

Greek:

> Nevertheless I would speak to the Lord;
> and argue before Him were it His pleasure.
>
> (13:3)

Hebrew:

> If only thou wouldst hide me in Sheol
> and conceal me till thy anger turns aside,
> if thou wouldst fix a limit for my time there,
> and then remember me! /
> Then I would not lose hope, however long my service
> waiting for my relief to come.
>
> (14:13-14)

Greek:

> (For though a man die he may be revived, after finishing the days of this life of his); I would wait patiently, until I come again into existence.
>
> (14:14)

In bulk, the changes in the Septuagint are relatively slight, but they are far from insignificant. The translator's theological approach to the poem leads him to depart from the Hebrew at points in the text where Job's piety, God's Providence, belief in the afterlife, or other matters of dogma are in doubt.

More immediately apparent at a first reading than these theological changes are the several details of plot which were modified or added outright in the translation from Hebrew to Greek. On the whole, these tend to shorten rather than to expand the poem, apparently reflecting the translator's desire to tighten it up a bit and hence increase its literary value. For what Samuel Johnson said of readers of *Paradise Lost*—"none ever have wished it longer than it is"—probably holds true for most readers of the Hebrew Book of Job. The Septuagint Job is only five-sixths the length of its exemplar, a disparity that was already noted by Origen in the third century, who observed that "often four or three verses, and sometimes fourteen or fifteen" are missing from the Greek.[51]

For the later history of the Job legend, the few additions to the plot of the Septuagint are more important than the omissions. In addition to the passage examined earlier which genealogizes Job and assures the reader that the biblical hero will be resurrected with other righteous men, in chapter 2 there are other important additions:

> Thereupon Satan withdrew from the presence of the Lord, and smote Job with foul ulcers from head to foot, / so that he took a shell to scrape away the ichor, and sat down on a dunghill[52] without the city. / And much time having elapsed, his wife said to him, How long wilt thou persist saying, Behold I will wait yet a little longer, in hope and expectation of my deliverance? For behold the memorial of thee—those sons and daughters, whom I brought forth with pangs and sorrow, and for whom I toiled in vain, are vanished from the earth; and thou thyself sittest among the putrifaction of worms, all night long in the open air, while I am wandering about, or working for wages, from place to place and from house to house, wishing for the setting of the sun, that I may rest from the labours and sorrows I endure. Do but say something for the Lord and die. / . . . Now when his three friends heard of all the calamities which were come upon him, they came to him each from his own country, namely, Eliphaz the king of the Thaimanites, Baldad the sovereign of the Saucheans, and Sophar the king of the Minaians.
>
> (2:7-9, 11)

In the expanded remarks of Job's wife, the translator has realized some of the dramatic possibilities inherent in her tantalizingly brief speech in the Hebrew. Here she vividly describes her own suffering as a result of Job's affliction. We learn for the first time that she has been reduced to the level of an itinerant domestic, much the same as Anna in the Book of Tobias. The passage also introduces three new minor motifs that are rapidly assimilated in the later history of the legend: Job's seat on a dunghill outside the city, his affliction with worms, and the royal status of his comforters (according to the Hebrew text, Job sat in ashes and we are not told that he departed from the city; we are not told that he was afflicted with worms; and his comforters are not identified as kings). It is of some interest to note that, except for the change from "ashes" to "dunghill," the Vulgate agrees with the Hebrew and not with the Greek, omitting any mention of Job's worms or the royal status of his comforters; and the King James follows the Hebrew exactly in all three cases.

That these and other motifs from the Septuagint nevertheless manage to find their way into numerous Western literary and visual renderings of Job's story reflects not so much the influence of the Septuagint alone as it reflects the larger influence of what I have been calling the "other biblical tradition of Job." This was a primarily oral folk tradition whose shadow we observe in the allusions to Job in Ezekiel, Tobias, and James; and some scholars think that, in either oral or possibly even in written form, it was a tradition available to the Septuagint translator of Job.[53] Thus, writing approximately a century later than Origen, Theodore, Bishop of Mopsuestia, testifies to the existence of an "outstanding and much esteemed history of the saintly Job, which circulated everywhere orally, in substantially the same form, not only amongst people of Jewish race but also amongst other peoples."[54] This "true" history Theodore contrasts with the Hebrew Book of Job, which he considers to be a fiction composed by a writer wishing to display his own skill. Job's speeches in the biblical story are, says Theodore, clearly unworthy of so virtuous a man, and the contest between Satan and God is obviously an author's fabrication.[55]

Although Theodore's views were not accepted by the Church, his testimony is further proof of the existence of a history of Job quite different from the one preserved in the Hebrew Bible. In this story God does not grant Satan power over Job because of a wager, and Job does not accuse God of injustice but instead looks forward with absolute and uncomplaining endurance to vindication and reward in the afterlife. The Septuagint in several respects reflects this other tradition of Job: there is a raising of Job's hope for and belief in an afterlife and a proportionate lowering and mitigation of his righteous rebelliousness. Whatever else may set it apart from the Hebrew poem, the shift in the weighting of these two principle motifs is the Septuagint Job's theological hallmark.

Job's hope for and belief in an afterlife—like his dunghill, his worms, and his royal comforters—is a motif that we shall meet at almost every turn in the Middle Ages. But there are milestones in the history of the Job legend, besides the Septuagint, in which the reweighting of the hope for an afterlife and righteous rebelliousness motifs is even more extreme, and in which new motifs are introduced, complicating and enriching the tradition in new and unexpected ways.

2 Apocryphal and Ecclesiastical Traditions

THE PSEUDEPIGRAPHAL *Testament of Job*—written in the first century B.C., perhaps by one of the Greek-speaking Therapeutae—tells a story about Job that differs markedly from the one in the Hebrew or Greek Bible.[1] The *Testament* is a fascinating work, and until recently a relatively neglected one, well worth studying for the lively story it tells and its occasional passages of great poetic power.[2] In addition many of its motifs find their way into medieval treatments of Job.

As the story begins, Job, who is dying, calls together his seven sons and three daughters (his second set) to tell them his life story and testament. He recounts his and his second wife's genealogy. His father was Esau and his wife is Dinah, daughter of Jacob; he also has a brother, Nahor, who is present to record the testament (51.1-3). Formerly Job was the ruler over all Egypt (28.8b) and lived near an idol to which people offered sacrifices. Job doubted that the idol could be God the Creator, and in a dream he was told by an angel that it was really the work of the devil. Job then resolved to destroy the idol, whereupon he was warned by an angel, in the name of the Lord, that if he did so he would suffer misfortune at the hands of Satan. The Lord also says to Job: "If you endure, I shall make your name renowned in all earthly generations until the consummation of the age. And I shall restore you once again to your possessions and you will receive a double payment, so that you may know that the Lord is impartial, rendering good things to each one who is obedient. And you will be raised up in the resurrection and you will be like an athlete who spars and endures hard labors and wins the crown." (4.6-8). When Job has destroyed the idol, Satan begins his assault. He comes to see Job disguised as a beggar asking for bread. Job sends him a burnt loaf—the doormaid out of pity substitutes a fresh loaf, but Satan rebukes her and demands the loaf that Job sent—and when he receives it he says: "As this loaf is wholly burnt, so I shall make your body. For within one hour I am going to depart and I will make you desolate" (7.10c-11); to which Job replies: "Do what you are going to do, whatever you plan to bring about. For I am prepared to undergo whatever you inflict on me" (7.12b-13).

Satan now obtains the Lord's permission to destroy Job's possessions, which are enumerated at great length and with special attention to their charitable use. For example, Job says: "Everyone from all regions began coming to meet me. And the four doors of my house were open. And I would command my house servants that the doors be open, since I was concerned lest anyone come seeking alms and see me sitting at the door and turn back ashamed, having taken nothing. But whenever they saw me sitting at one door they could exit through the other and take as much as they might need. And I had thirty special tables in my house reserved at all hours for strangers only" (9.6-10.1). And again:

> And those who milked the cows were at a loss, since milk flowed on the mountains, and butter spread over my roads from its abundance [cp. Job 29:6]. They bedded down in the rocks and in the mountains on account of the young being born. And because of this, the mountains were gushing milk and became as congealed butter. And my servants, who were in charge of the food of the widows and the poor, grew tired. And they would curse me with contempt, saying, Who will provide for us from his meats that we might be filled? Yet I was exceedingly kind! And I used to have six harps[3] and a ten-stringed lyre. And I would arise daily after the widows were fed and I would take the lyre and play for them [the servants], and they [the widows] would chant. And by means of the psaltery I would remind them [the widows] of God so that they might glorify the Lord. And if my maid-

servants ever began murmuring, I would take up the psaltery and play for them the payment of recompense. And I would make them stop murmuring in contempt.

(13.1-14.5)

We now hear how Satan destroyed most of Job's cattle, while Job's countrymen ran off with the remainder; then Satan led a Persian army in plundering Job's house and killed Job's children by toppling a house down on them. Finally, seeing that even after all this Job was still uncomplainingly steadfast, Satan obtained the Lord's permission to afflict Job's body. As Job describes it:

> And then the Lord delivered me into his hands to deal with my body as he wished, but he did not give him authority over my soul. And he came to me as I was sitting on my throne . . . and he was like a great hurricane and overturned my throne. And I spent three hours under my throne unable to leave. And he struck me with a cruel disease from the top of my head to the soles of my feet. And in great confusion and distress I left the city, and as I sat on the dungheap my body was infested by worms. And discharges from my body also combined to drench the ground with their moisture. There were many worms in it and if a worm fell off, I would pick it up and return it to the same place, saying: Stay in the same place in which you were put until you receive instructions from the one who commanded you.
>
> (20.3-10b)

Job's wife, whose name was Sitidos, then had to find work as a maidservant to obtain bread, which she divided with her incapacitated husband. When it became harder and harder for her to find work, she took to begging for bread in the marketplace, whereupon Satan disguised himself as a breadseller and tricked her into letting him shear her hair in public and take it in exchange for bread. When she informs Job of her encounter with the breadseller, in the course of a lengthy lament for her fallen estate and vanished prosperity, Job rebukes her and, quite unexpectedly, orders Satan to come out from behind her: "Come to the front, stop hiding yourself! Does the lion show his strength in a cage? Does the fledgling take flight while in a basket? Is this not useless? I say, Come out and battle with me!" (27.1b-2c). At which point Satan comes out from behind Job's wife and, weeping, admits that he has been vanquished:

> See, Job, I am distraught and I yield to you who are of human flesh—I who am spirit. You have a disease, while I am greatly disturbed. I became like an athlete wrestling with another athlete, and one threw the other down. And the one above silenced the one underneath by filling his mouth with sand and mangling every limb of the one who was underneath him. And when the latter exhibited perseverance and did not become distraught, the one above gave a loud cry of surrender. So you, Job, were underneath and diseased, but you overcame my wrestling holds which I applied to you.
>
> (27.3b-8)

With that, Satan departs from Job for three years.

Job at this point interrupts his narrative to say: "Now then, my children, you also must be patient in everything that happens to you, for patience is superior to everything" (27.10).

Twenty years after the onset of his illness, four kings, Eliphaz, Elious, Baldas, and Sophar, come to visit Job. Because of the stench of his body, they approach with fragrant substances in their hands and order the soldiers who accompany them to fumigate the area with incense. They lament at great length the fallen splendor of Job's throne and repeatedly state their unwillingness to believe that the man they see on the dunghill is the Job they knew of old. Job's reply is a hymn praising the heavenly throne and denigrating earthly kingship. The kings are angered, and Baldas asks Job: "If you place your hope in God, how then does he act unjustly when he judges, inflicting on you these maladies or taking away your possessions? If he also took it away, it would have been better for him not to give anything. A king never punishes his own soldier who serves him well. Or who can ever comprehend the deep things of the Lord and his wisdom so that someone dares to ascribe to the Lord an injustice?" (37.5b-8); to which Job replies, in part: "For who are we to be busying ourselves with heavenly matters, seeing that we are fleshly and have our lot in dust and ashes? Therefore, in order that you may know that my heart is composed, listen to what I ask you: Food through the mouth, and then water through the mouth is swallowed in the same throat. But when the two fall into the latrine, they are then separated from each other. Who then divides them?" (38.8b). Sophar then offers Job a chance to be treated by physicians that he and his fellow kings have brought along. Job replies: "My healing and treatment are from the Lord, who created even the physicians" (38.13b).

Now Job's wife, Sitidos, approaches and pleads with the four kings to dig through the rubble of the house in which her children perished, so that they may receive proper burial. Job forbids this, asserting that his children have already been taken up to heaven. And when the kings take this as a sign of Job's madness, Job grants them and his wife a vision in which they see the children "crowned alongside the splendor of the heavenly one" (40.5), after which Sitidos goes off and dies peacefully.

But the kings continue their harangue until the Lord appears through a tempest, censures Elious (in whom, Job learns, it was a "beast" and not "man" who spoke), rebukes the three other kings, and then forgives them after Job offers sacrifices in their behalf. Eliphaz now recites a hymn condemning Elious, "the one of darkness and not of light" (43.42). Job returns to the city where his friends each give him a lamb and a gold coin and the Lord blesses his possessions and doubles them.

His narrative over, Job turns to his children and says: "And now, my children, behold I am dying. Above all do not forget the Lord. Do good to the poor, do not overlook the helpless. Do not take wives for yourselves from foreigners. Behold then, my children, I shall divide all my possessions among you, so each of you has legal control and each has the resources to do good works unhindered from his share" (45.1-5). He then proceeds to divide his property among his sons; and when his daughters complain, Job reassures them that they shall have an even better inheritance, whereupon he brings forth from three golden boxes, "three bands, shimmering, so that no man could describe their form, since they are not from earth but are from heaven, flashing with bright sparks like rays of the sun" (46.8). Of the origin and special virtues of these bands Job says:

> Not only will you sustain life from these, but these bands will also lead you into the better world, to live in the heavens. Are you ignorant, then, my children, of the value of these cords, of which the Lord considered me worthy on the day on which he wished to have mercy on me and remove from my body the diseases and the worms? When he called me he set before me these three bands and said to me: Arise, gird your loins like a man! I shall question you, and you answer me. So I took them and girded myself, and immediately the worms disappeared from my body and the plagues as well. And then, through the Lord, my body grew strong as if it had not suffered anything at all. But I could even forget the pains in my heart! And the lord spoke to me by a powerful act, showing me things present and things to come. Now then, my children, since you have them you will not have the enemy opposing you at all, neither will you have anxieties about him in your mind, because it is a protective amulet of the Lord. Rise, then, gird them around you before I die in order that you may be able to see those who are coming for my departure, so that you may marvel at the creatures of God.
>
> (47.3b-12)

When the three daughters don the bands, they suddenly begin to chant "in the angelic language" (48.3). Three days later, Job and his daughters see "those who had come for his soul" (52.2). To one of his daughters Job gives a lyre, to a second a censer, to the third a kettledrum.

Now Job's soul is taken up in a chariot and his body is borne to its tomb, while his daughters, girded about and singing hymns to God, lead the way: "And at once all the widows and orphans circled about him, preventing him from being brought into the tomb. And after three days they laid him in the tomb as if in a beautiful sleep, since he had received a name renowned in all generations forever" (53.5-6).

On first impression the *Testament* may seem fairly chaotic, a work brim-full of loosely articulated comings and goings, marvels, disguises, hymns, mystical flights, and visions. However, beneath its episodic structure there is a unifying action. In the first half of the work this action is a struggle—

or, as it is described in a particularly effective passage, a kind of wrestling match—between Job and Satan, the paragon of endurance pitted against the Evil One himself. Having defeated Satan, in the second half of the work Job continues to struggle, this time against the four kings who visit him, and in particular against Elious, who, because he is later identified as an agent of the Evil One, links Job's struggle in the second half of the work with his struggle in the first. This underlying structure of conflict, similar to the structure of the Book of Job, where Job first endures the onslaught of Satan then of his comforters, is only one of several continuities between the *Testament* and the biblical Job tradition.[4] For the most part, however, it was not the affinities of the *Testament* to the Bible but rather its distinctive features, its reweighting of biblical motifs and its introduction of numerous nonbiblical ones, which were to influence later legends of Job.

The *Testament*, as its title implies, is cast in the form of a Last Will and Testament, a type of narrative that flourished in Judeo-Christian literature of the intertestamental period and for centuries thereafter.[5] In the usual format, a testament opens with a passage in which the testator, near death, gives his name and lineage and gathers around him those whom he wishes to address, usually his children. There then follows a narrative of the testator's life, most often stressing a single virtue or a besetting sin, followed by ethical instruction, an eschatological section, and a description of the testator's death and burial.

For the most part the *Testament* follows this format, except that its narrative section is longer than usual and the explicit ethical instruction section, which consists of only a few verses, is shorter than usual; in addition, the distribution of Job's wealth—that is, his property to his sons and his magical bands to his daughters—seems to have replaced the usual eschatological section. The *Testament* also includes more hymns and poetical speeches than are usually present in testamentary literature—one imaginative critic has suggested that these poetical speeches may indeed have been presented dramatically at a community gathering of the Therapeutae[6] —but it has far fewer speeches than either the Hebrew or Greek biblical story of Job.

Like the Septuagint Job, however, it shows a tendency

toward literary embellishment and thematic simplification quite uncharacteristic of the Hebrew. Probably the most self-consciously "literary" feature of the *Testament* is its use of similes (of an athlete, 4.8b; a woman in labor, 18.5; a sea-tossed merchant, 18.6; and a pair of wrestlers, 27.5-8). In addition, it provides Job's children with fanciful, mythologically suggestive names and includes a number of other striking images and poetic expressions which "have both in matter and in manner, a suggestion of the influence of Greek literature."[7] Of its links with the Septuagint, the most prominent are Job's removal to a dunghill, his worms, the royal status of his comforters, his belief in resurrection, and the expanded role of his wife (which is even more strikingly similar to the role of Anna in the Book of Tobias).[8] Despite these points of contact, however, it would be a serious mistake to overlook the many departures of the *Testament* from the biblical Job tradition.

In the opening passage of the work, Job is identified as a son of Esau and husband of Dinah, and later on we learn that he was ruler over all Egypt. Of these three details placing Job in the patriarchal period of biblical history, none appears in the Hebrew Bible, and only the first puts the *Testament* in rough agreement with the Septuagint, where Job is said to have been the grandson, not the son, of Esau. In light of this genealogy, Job's advice to his children to avoid intermarriage, which strongly implies that he is an Israelite, is a bit puzzling. (But it may help to explain why medieval writers often took Job to be an Israelite, thereby eliminating an important motif of the biblical story, namely, the indeterminacy of Job's race.) For other accounts of Job's marriage to Dinah and his connection with Egypt we must look not to the Bible but to rabbinic legend, where we also find analogues to Job's address to his worms, his anti-idolatrous iconoclasm, and his great charity.[9]

In the warning and promise delivered to Job by the angel, we find an early statement of the major thematic premises of the *Testament*, premises very different from those in the biblical story. To begin with, the powerful dramatic ironies of the biblical story are altogether eliminated. Here Job knows from the outset exactly what is happening to him. The theologically vexing wager between the Lord and Satan is gone. There is no doubt about the origin of Job's suffering, for by directly antagonizing Satan he has brought it upon himself. He knows that it is only his body that can suffer and that his soul is safe. Similarly, there is no doubt about Job's reward. As he learns from the angel, it will include immortal fame, material restoration of twice what he has lost, and resurrection. These are themes found also in the Septuagint, and less explicitly in the Hebrew Job, but there they are handled very differently. Furthermore, several important motifs in the biblical story have been dropped from the *Testament*, including what are among the most problematic theologically but also among the most profound: vindicatory suffering, the purgative and pedagogical purposes of righteous suffering, and righteous rebelliousness.

In the constant and unequivocal stress that the *Testament* places on Job's perfect patience and endurance, we find the first solid basis for those allusions to an unstintingly patient Job that we came across in Ezekiel, Tobias, and James. Here Job becomes, as the imagery of the *Testament* would have it, an athlete or wrestler *for* God; he is no longer the righteous rebel *against* God whom we meet in the Bible.[10] And with similar effect, in the debates between Job and the four kings which take up most of the second half of the *Testament*, there is a complete reversal of the positions held in the biblical dialogues. Thus, in the *Testament* it is Job who upholds the notion of divine justice, a few times even echoing the divine speeches from the Book of Job in the process (38.1-8), while it is his interlocutors who are besieged by doubts. The reversal is perhaps most evident in the case of Elious, whose counterpart in the biblical story, Elihu, is thoroughly pious, but who is portrayed in the *Testament* as a demonic figure, a beast in disguise (42.1).

Of less profound thematic significance but of great importance for later representations of Job, especially in art, are the references in the *Testament* to women and to music, the latter always with positive associations, the former usually with negative ones. For example, Job's doormaid acts on a generous but misdirected impulse and his maidservants murmur "in contempt." And this antifeminist motif is repeated and given greater prominence in the portrayal of Job's wife, who sustains her husband by begging for bread and sharing it with him, but not without berating him and being easily deceived by Satan along the way. Only Job's daughters, who gain enlightenment under their father's, not their mother's, guidance, are seen in an entirely positive light. On the other hand, the role of music in the *Testament* is consistently positive: Job plays instruments and sings to cheer up his servants and educate the beneficiaries of his charity in the love of God (14.1-5); and later he gives two of his daughters musical instruments as gifts (52.2).

In addition to the expanded role of women and the importance of music, another nonbiblical motif in the *Testament* that was to play a role in medieval representations of Job is the presence of physicians. Although we never actually see them, we learn of their presence when Sophar offers Job their services and Job refuses, declaring instead that he prefers to be treated and healed by God, "who created even the physicians" (38.9-13).

Another point on which the *Testament* contradicts the Hebrew and Septuagint Bibles is the distribution of Job's possessions to his heirs. Whereas the biblical versions draw our attention to the unusual fact that Job's daughters shared equally with their brothers of their father's wealth,[11] the author of the *Testament* seems to go out of his way to deny this. Instead, he recounts how Job awards his property to his sons, and to each of his daughters, when they complain of the inequity, he awards one of the magical bands he received from the Lord in the theophany. These bands, Job explains, are far more valuable than any of his other possessions, for they were the instruments that effected his cure from the worms and the plagues; they also act as all-purpose protective amulets against Satan and as talismans enabling the bearer "to live in the heavens" (47.3). Although this is not a theme that medieval authors who treat Job adopt, the importance of amulets of this sort in medieval literature and life—the green girdle in *Sir Gawain and the Green Knight* is a prime instance—is a well established fact (see fig. 8).

One reason that the author may have felt obliged to develop the theme of the magical bands was to make up for the failure of the biblical narrator to mention how Job was healed. Nowhere in the Book of Job, either Hebrew or Septuagint, are we told that as a part of his vindication and material restoration Job was cured of the disease or diseases with which Satan afflicted him—we merely assume that he was. Since one of his goals appears to have been to rationalize and smooth obscurities of the biblical narrative, the author of the *Testament* may have introduced the magical bands to make up for this small but disturbing omission.

Another reason, and the more compelling one, I think, was the author's desire to portray Job as an initiate capable of initiating others in the secrets of the heavenly throne.[12] The magic and mystical flights in the *Testament* were undoubtedly very appealing to the Therapeutae or whoever else the original audience of the work may have been, but in later works about Job their significance is slight. Nevertheless, it is not that uncommon to find Job represented in later ages as a wise man, a prophet, or even a philosopher. And although there is sufficient basis for this portrayal of Job in the biblical and ecclesiastical traditions—for example, in the Wisdom Poem in chapter 28 of the Book of Job itself or in the "prophecies" attributed to Job by later exegetical writers—we should not be too quick to rule out the possibility that the portrait of Job's magical powers in the *Testament* contributed to its survival.

Having surveyed the major landmarks in the biblical and apocryphal traditions of Job, we now have a more or less recognizable composite picture of the Job story as it was known to the artists and writers of the Middle Ages. For some important details, however, we must consider a third major source of medieval Job-lore, namely, the enormous body of patristic and later exegetical writings in which the story of Job so frequently figures. Because this material has been treated in detail (although far from exhaustively) by a number of scholars, for our present purpose it will be sufficient to identify only those prominent exegetical themes that find their way into medieval literary and visual representations of Job. These are found for the most part in Gregory the Great's sixth-century *Moralia in Iob* (*Morals on the*

Book of Job), a work unrivaled in its influence on Christian interpretation of Job in the Middle Ages and for a long time thereafter.[13]

Gregory began work on the *Moralia* sometime between 579 and 585, while he was papal nuncio in Constantinople; but it was not until 595, when he was already five years into his tenure of the Roman see, that the work was finally completed.[14] For Rome, as for Gregory personally, these were difficult times. As Laistner writes:

> Few men placed in a position of the highest authority have lived through times as difficult and troubled as were the fourteen years during which Gregory occupied the chair of Peter . . . Frequent plagues and famines and the constant attacks of the Lombards drained Italy of her people and her resources, and entailed frightful misery for the survivors . . . Even a robust man might have quailed at the labour and the responsibility. Gregory fulfilled his high destiny with such success that his papacy became a model for future incumbents in the Roman see; in addition he found some time for authorship, although throughout his tenure of the papacy to his death in 604 he was constantly racked by a painful malady.
>
> (pp. 103-104)

Like the age in which he lived, Gregory was apparently ripe for Job. And as the following quotation from his prefatory *Epistle to Leander* reveals, when Gregory decided to write a commentary on the Book of Job he did so to a large extent because he felt a particular affinity to its protagonist:

> For many a year's circuit has gone by since I have been afflicted with frequent pains in the bowels, and the powers of my stomach being broken down, makes me at all times and seasons weakly; and under the influence of fevers, slow, but in constant succession, I draw my breath with difficulty; and when in the midst of these sufferings I ponder with earnest heed, that according to the testimony of Scripture, *He scourgeth every son whom He receiveth;* the more I am weighed down by the severity of present afflictions, from my anticipations for eternity, I gather strength to breathe with so much the better assurance. And perchance it was this that Divine Providence designed, that I a stricken one, should set forth Job stricken, and that by these

> scourges I should the more perfectly enter into the feelings of one that was scourged.
>
> (*Moralia*, I, 10)

Earlier in the same epistle we learn that Gregory decided to structure the *Moralia* as he has done at the insistence and for the benefit of his monkish brethren in Constantinople. As he explains, they wanted him

> to set forth the book of blessed Job; and as far as the Truth should inspire me with powers, to lay open to them those mysteries of such depth; and they made this too an additional burden which their petition laid upon me, that I would not only unravel the words of the history in allegorical senses, but that I would go on to give to the allegorical senses the turn of a moral exercise, with the addition of somewhat yet harder, that I would crown the several meanings with testimonies, and that the testimonies, which I brought forward, should they chance to appear involved, should be disentangled by the aid of additional explanation.
>
> (I, 4-5)

With this as his interpretative methodology—a somewhat elaborated version of the exegetical methodology he had inherited mainly from Augustine[15]—Gregory set out, in the course of six volumes and thirty-five books, to interpret every verse in the Book of Job, stressing now the literal or historical level, now the allegorical level, and now the moral level, and occasionally interpreting a verse on all three levels (I,7). Of the three levels of interpretation, the allegorical is probably the most distinctively marked and hence easiest to identify: any verse in the Book of Job which Gregory considers to be "typical" (I, 7), that is, which he takes to refer to Christ or the Church, is being treated allegorically. For example, here is Gregory's allegorical commentary on Job 1:21, "Naked came I out of my mother's womb, and naked shall I return thither": "The mother of our Redeemer, after the flesh, was the Synagogue, from whom He came forth to us, made manifest by a Body . . . when He issued from the flesh of the Synagogue He came openly manifest to the Gentiles . . . the time will doubtless come in the end of the world, when He will make Himself known, even as He is God, to the remnant of His people. Whence it is likewise justly said in this place, *and naked shall I return thither*" (I, 109). Taken allegorically, then, this verse is about Jesus' first and second comings, not about Job.

To illustrate the difference between Gregory's historical and moral commentary—a difference that is hard to appreciate from a modern perspective—here are, respectively, his historical and moral commentaries on Job 3:3, "Let the day perish wherein I was born":

> For what is to be understood by 'the day of our birth,' save the whole period of our mortal state? So long as this keeps us fast in the corruptions of this our mutable state of being, the unchangeableness of eternity does not appear to us. He, then, who already beholds the day of eternity, endures with difficulty the day of his mortal being. And observe, he saith not, 'Let the day perish wherein I was created,' but, *let the day perish wherein I was born.* For man was created in a day of righteousness, but now he is born in a time of guilt; for Adam was created, but Cain was the first man that was born. What then is it to curse the day of his birth, but to say plainly, 'May the day of change perish, and the light of eternity burst forth?'
>
> (I, 186)

> It seems as it were like day, when the good fortune of this world smiles upon us, but it is a day that ends in night, for temporal prosperity often leads to the darkness of affliction . . . by 'the day' may be understood the pleasure of sin.
>
> (I, 200)

Without checking back to see which is which, most readers, I think, would be hard put to say which of the latter two passages is the historical or literal interpretation of Job 3:3 and which the moral or nonliteral one.[16]

Another example of Gregory's approach to Job is his comment on Job 38:2, "Who is this that wrappeth up sentences in unskilful words?" the first verse in the Lord's answer to Job out of the whirlwind: "As we have said also in the former part, an interrogative of this kind, in which it is said, *Who is this?* is the beginning of a reproof. For Elihu had spoken arrogantly . . . Having then glanced with contempt on this man

[Elihu!], His words are directed to the instruction of Job" (III, 268-269). Though the Lord's words in Job 38:2 are clearly aimed at Job, Gregory, by sheer exegetical main force, deflects them onto Elihu.

As these passages and scores of others show, Gregory's exegetical method enabled him to by-pass contradictory or otherwise vexing verses in the Book of Job and to reconstitute the story of Job into a comprehensive statement on Christian dogma and morality. Thus, Gregory at one point argues in favor of the Deuteronomist theory of justice, while denying its applicability in the case of Job (I, 321-322). Similarly, because he is more concerned with the elucidation of Christian doctrine than with the faithful representation of what he regarded as superficial contradictions in the Book of Job, Gregory gives scarcely any weight at all to the theme of Job's righteous rebelliousness—a theme to which, incidentally, Gregory's fourth-century predecessor, Ambrose, pays fairly close attention.[17] As a result, the portrait of Job that emerges in the *Moralia* is a double image: on the historical and moral levels it is the portrait of a patient Christian saint, and on the allegorical level, the portrait of a type or prefiguration of Christ—representations of Job that, to alter the metaphor slightly, are really silhouettes of the many-sided biblical figure.[18]

Nevertheless, while expounding a systematic theology, Gregory does manage to offer numerous opinions about the Job story that, together with his silhouettes of Job as a patient Christian saint and a type of Christ, were to exert a powerful influence on the medieval iconography and literary history of Job. These include the belief that Job was attacked by the devil, by his wife, who was instigated by the devil, and by his comforters, who—especially Elihu—were also put to their work by the devil;[19] that Job fought back like a true athlete or warrior of God;[20] that Job had perfect faith in the resurrection and afterlife;[21] and that just as Job is a type of Christ, so the monstrous beasts named in the Lord's speeches, Behemoth and Leviathan, are types of the devil.[22] Though all of these motifs are found in earlier exegetical writing—and some were already present in the Septuagint and the *Testament of Job*—no single work as influential as the *Moralia* includes them all.

Whatever its critical merits or deficiencies, for almost one thousand years the *Moralia* was the best known and most authoritative commentary on the Book of Job in Western Christendom. More than just a commentary on Job, it was also one of the most important compendia of Christian doctrine to be had, as few medieval libraries were without it.[23] To quote Spicq: "the Middle Ages, from the outset at least, follows the principles of St. Augustine and the practice of St. Gregory, or St. Augustine through the *Moralia* of St. Gregory" (p. 11; my translation). Thus, the *Glossa ordinaria*, departing from its usual procedure of drawing on several commentaries, includes a summary of the *Moralia* as its gloss on the Book of Job. In addition, there are epitomes and translations of the *Moralia* by Notker Labeo, Odo of Cluny, Peter Damian, Bruno of Asti, Rupert of Deutz, Peter of Blois, and many others. The *Moralia* is also the source of the poem on Job in Peter Riga's extraordinarily popular *Aurora*, as it is the source of numerous iconographic motifs (see figs. 12-15).[24] Only with the coming of scholasticism and the commentaries on Job by Albert the Great and Aquinas, culminating in the more literal exegesis of Job by Nicholas of Lyra in the fourteenth century, did the absolute dominance of the *Moralia* begin to wane.[25]

Among the questions that Gregory and other exegetical writers considered were the Book of Job's authorship, genre, and verse form. As Datz and Lewalski have shown, beginning with Origen and down to Milton's day and beyond there was a diversity of opinion as to whether Moses, Job, Elihu, Solomon, or one of the Prophets was the author of the Book of Job.[26] On the other hand, starting with Jerome, it was almost unanimously agreed that, except for the prose prologue and epilogue, the verse form of Job was hexameter "running in dactyl and spondee"; and for well over a thousand years after Jerome exegetes and other writers point to these so-called hexameters as evidence of the poem's epic character (though the view that Job is a drama also had its early exponents and was to gain favor steadily).[27]

The role of Job in the liturgy of the Catholic Church also helped shape his image and insure his popularity, not only in the Middle Ages but up to the present day. Job had, and still has, an important function in the service known as the Office of the Dead. From small beginnings in the early history of the Church, this office came to occupy a prominent place among liturgical observances of medieval clergy and laity. Thus, starting in the eighth century, the Office of the Dead was recited with increasing frequency, first in monasteries, then in cathedrals, and finally among secular clergy and the devout everywhere.[28] By the fourteenth century, and in England in particular, with outbreaks of plague in 1349 and periodically thereafter throughout the century, there was no shortage of opportunities for a cleric to supplement his income by reciting the Office of the Dead or other memorial services. As the Dreamer in *Piers Plowman* explains:

> . . . ich lyue in Londene and on Londen bothe;
> The lomes ["tools"] þat ich laboure with and lyflode deserue
> Ys *Paternoster*, and my Prymer, *Placebo* and *Dirige*,
> And my Sauter som tyme, and my Seuene Psalmes.
> Thus ich synge for hure soules of suche as me helpen . . .
> (C-Text, VI, 46-50)

Chaucer, too, in his portrait of the Parson, refers to the recitation of memorial services for pay as a common practice, indeed, an abuse, of which the Parson is not guilty (*Canterbury Tales*, A 507-510). And Wyclif also inveighed against the Office of the Dead, as against all other accretions to the liturgy which might keep priests from studying Scripture and preaching to the flock.[29]

What, then, was the shape of this very popular office? And how and where did Job figure in it? For several reasons, like most liturgical texts of the Middle Ages, the Office of the Dead varied considerably from place to place, not only from country to country but from church to church; we cannot speak of a single Office of the Dead in the Latin Middle Ages. Second, the role of Job in the office varied considerably over time as well as from place to place. To consider only the extremes: while the second-century worshiper who recited the memorial prayer known as Commendatio Animae (out of which the Office of the Dead is supposed to have grown) merely asked: "Deliver us as you have delivered Job," his counterpart a thousand years later, reciting the Office of the Dead, read out dozens of verses from the Book of Job.[30] We do not know precisely how the Office of the Dead developed from earlier memorial services or how Job's role in it grew.[31] But we do know that Job is the principal biblical figure in the fully developed Office of the Dead of the High Middle Ages and after. And by the late eleventh century the text of the office in use at Salisbury Cathedral, the so-called Sarum Use, had gained wide acceptance and had what amounted to official recognition from Rome.[32]

The Sarum Office of the Dead consists of prayers for three canonical hours: vespers, matins, and lauds. The matins of the office was commonly referred to as Dirige (whence English "dirge"), after the first word of its opening antiphon: "Dirige Domine Deus meus in conspectu tuo viam meam" (Ps. 5:9). And in the same way the vespers of the office was called Placebo, after its opening antiphon: "Placebo Domine in regione vivorum" (Ps. 114:9). Sometimes in the manuscripts, however, Dirige refers to both vespers and matins together, probably because in the long summer nights matins was moved back to follow vespers, and so the two offices were recited consecutively.[33] Similarly, Dirige sometimes refers to matins and lauds of the office, because they were regularly recited consecutively.

Our interest here, however, is in the Dirige proper, that is, Matins of the Dead, which includes all those passages from Job—nine "lessons" in all—that are found in the Office of the Dead. This is the longest of the three "hours" of the office, long enough in fact to be divided into three nocturns or sections, which would normally be recited at 9:00 P.M., midnight, and 3:00 A.M. In the first nocturn the verses recited were Job 7:16-21, 10:1-7, and 10:8-12; in the second nocturn, 13:23-28, 14:1-6, and 14:13-16; and in the third nocturn, 17:1-3, 17:11-15, 19:20-27, and 10:18-22.

In a liturgical setting, then, and in a drastically abbreviated format, the Book of Job was experienced *daily* by medieval clergy and laity, who recited the Divine Office and those additional prayers, like Matins of the Dead, sanctioned by the Sarum Use. In France and England the nine lessons from

Job in the liturgy eventually came to be known as "le petit Job" and "Pety Job," and they were frequently the subject of vernacular verse paraphrase. Most people in the Middle Ages would have had direct access to the Book of Job only through these verses.

Perhaps the best way to get a sense of how this "little Job" portrayed the biblical figure is to read it precisely as it came to be read in the later Middle Ages, namely, as a shorter version of the Book of Job. The text below is from an early fifteenth-century English primer, following the Sarum Use. That "little Job" is found in the English primer, the layman's prayer book, as well as in Latin service books, indicates how widely available this version of the Job story was, compared to the much less accessible complete version in the Vulgate. So as not to lose sight of the liturgical context, I have indicated in square brackets the major biblical texts which make up the rest of the office:[34]

[Psalms 5-7]

leccio .1ª. Parce michi domine!

Lord, spare þou me, for my daies ben not! / what is man, for þou magnefiest him? eþer what settest þou þin herte towardis him? / þou visitist him eerli; and sodeynli þou preuest him. / hou longe sparest þou not me, neþer suffrest þat y swolewe my spotele? / y haue synned, o þou keper of men, what shal y do to þee? whi hast þou set me contrarie to þee? & y am maad greuouse to my silf? / whi doist þou not awey my synne? & whi takest þou not a-wey my wickidnesse? lo, now, y slepe in poudur; and if þou sekest me eerli, y schal not abide.

(Job 7:16-21)

Leccio iiª: Tedet animam.

It anoieþ my soule of my lyif; y schal lette my speche aȝenes me, y schal speke in þe bitternesse of my soule. / y schal seie to god, 'nyle þou condempne me; schewe þou to me whi þou demest me so. / whe þer it semeþ good to þee, if þou falseli chalengist & oppressist me, þe werk of þin hondis, & if þou helpe þe counseil of wickid men. / wheþer fleischli iȝen ben to þee? eþer as a man seeþ, also þou schalt se? / wheþer þi daies ben as þe daies of man; & þi ʒeeris ben as mannes tymes, / þat þou enquere my wickidnesse, & enserche my synne, / & wite þat y haue do no wickid þing, siþen no man is þat mai delyuere fro þyn hond?'

(Job 10:1-7)

leccio iij[a]: Manus tue.

Thyne hondis maden me, & han formed me al in cumpas; & þou castist me doun so sodeynli! / y biseche þee haue þou mynde þat þou madist me of cley, & schalt brynge me aʒen in-to poudur. / wheþer þou hast not softid me as mylk; and hast cruddid me to-gideres as chese? / þou hast cloþid me wiþ skyn and flesch; & þou hast ioyned me to-gideres wiþ bones and synewes. / þou hast ʒoue liyf and merci to me; & þi visitacioun haþ kept my spirit.

(Job 10:8-12)

[Psalms 22, 24, 27]

leccio iiij[a]: Quantas habeo.

Hou grete synnes & wickidnessis haue y! schewe to me my felonyes & trespassis! / whi hidest þou þi face, & demest me, þin enemy? / þou schewist þi power aʒenes a leef which is rauyschid wiþ þe wynde, & þou pursuest drie stobil; / for þou writist bitternessis aʒenes me, & wolt waste me wiþ þe synnes of my waxinge age. / þou hast set my foot in a stok, and þou hast kepte alle my paþþis, & þou hast biholde þe steppis of my feet; / & y schal be wastid as rotenesse, & as a cloþ which is etun of a mouʒte.

(Job 13:23-28)

leccio v[a]: Homo natus de muliere.

A man þat is born of a womman, lyueþ schort tyme, & is fillid wiþ many wrecchidnessis. / which goiþ out & is defoulid as a flour, & fleeþ as a schadewe, & dwelliþ neuer parfitli in þe same staat. / and gessist þou it worþi to opene þin iʒen on siche a man, & to brynge him into doom wiþ þee? / who mai make him clene þat is conseyued of vnclene seed? wheþer not þou þat aloon? / þe daies of a man ben schorte; þe noumbre of his moneþis ben at þee; þou hast set hise termes, þe whiche moun not be passid. / þer-for go þou awey fro him a littil, þat he haue reste, til þe mede disirid come; & his dai is as þe dai of an hirid man.

(Job 14:1-6)

leccio vj[a]: [Quis michi hoc tribuat].

Who mai graunte to me þis, þat þou defende me in helle, & hide me til þi greet veniaunce passe, & þat þou ordeyne me a tyme in which þou haue mynde of me? / gessist þou not þat a deed man schal lyue a ʒen? / Alle þe daies in whiche y trauele now, y abide til my chaungyng come. / þou schalt clepe me, & y schal answere þee; þou schalt strecche þi riʒt hond to þe werk of þin hondis. / sikirli þou hast noumbrid my steppis; but lord, spare þou my synnes!

(Job 14:13-16)

[Psalms 39-41]

leccio vij[a]: Spiritus meus.

Mi spirit schal be maad feble; my daies schulen be maad schort; & oneli þe sepulcre is left to me. / y haue not synned; and ʒit myn iʒe dwelliþ in bitternessis. / lord, deliuere þou me, & sette þou me bisides þee; and þe hond of whom euere þou wolt, fiʒte aʒenes me! . . . Mi daies ben passid. my þouʒtis ben scaterid, turmentynge myn herte. / þei han turned þe niʒt in-to dai; and efte aftir derknessis, y hope liʒt. / if y susteyne, helle is myn hous; & y haue araied my bed in derknessis. / I seide to rotenesse: 'þou art my fadir'; & to wormes, ʒe ben my modir & my sister'; / þerfore, where is now myn abidyng, & my pacience? my lord god, þou it ert!

(Job 17:1-3, 11-15)

leccio viij: pelli mee.

Whanne my fleisch was wastid, my boon cleuyde to my skyn, & oneli lippis ben left aboute my teeþ. / haue ʒe merci on me, haue ye merci on me; nameli, ʒe my frendis! for þe hond of þe lord haþ touchid me. / whi pursue ʒe me as god doiþ, & ben fillid wiþ my fleschis? / who mai graunte me þat my wordis be writun? who mai graunte me þat þei be writun in a bok, / wiþ an yrun poyntel, eþer wiþ a plate of leed, eþer wiþ a chisel be grauun in a flynt? / ffor y wot þat myn aȝenbier lyueþ; & in þe laste dai y schal rise fro þe erþe, / & eft y schal be cumpassid wiþ my skyn; & in my flesch y schal se god my saueour. / whom y my silf schal se, & myn iȝen schulen biholde, beynge not anoþir: þis is myn hope, & kept in my bosum.

(Job 19:20-27)

leccio ix[a]: Quare de vulua, & cetera.

Whi brouȝtest þou me forþ fro þe wombe? wolde god þat y hadde be wastid, þat noon iȝe hadde seie me! / þanne had y be as þouȝ y hadde not be; fro þe wombe ybore to þe graue. / wheþer þe fewenesse of my daies schal not be endid in schort tyme? lord! suffre þou me, þat y weile a litil while my sorewe, / or y wende hennes, þat y turne not aȝen, to þe derklond, & keuerid wiþ þe derknesse of deeþ; / þe lond of wrecchidnesse and of derknesse, where þe schadewe of deeþ, & noon ordre, but euerlasting [g]risnesse dwelliþ inne.

(Job 10:18-22)

If each lesson were not identified in the primer by chapter and verse, we would probably not notice that the last is out of biblical order. All nine are spoken by Job, they are not linked in any obvious progression, and none is earmarked by any narrative detail. Sometimes the English follows the Latin so closely it ends up being obscure (for example, 10:1); other times the English departs from the Vulgate wording or word order, with varying consequences. For the Vulgate's "nihil" in Job 7:16, for example, the primer text reads "not," which hardly makes sense unless it is a phonetic spelling of "nought." But the reading does not affect our overall understanding of the passage. On the whole it is quite clear, while close to the proximate Latin original. Job is contrite, he confesses that he has sinned, and he prays for remission of his sins and wickedness. He is univocal, and sounds very much like the author of those psalms which precede the texts from Job in the office, especially Psalm 6, one of the so-called penitential psalms.

In the second lesson, however, there is a reversal. Job complains that he is not guilty of sin, that God has been unfair. Again the English follows the Latin original fairly closely.

But one significant departure is the translation of Latin "Noli" in verse 2 as the Middle English "nyle," that is, the substitution of a future for an imperative, with a slight softening of Job's plea as a result. And a softening of Job's tone seems also to be the intended effect of translating "peccatis adolescentiae meae" in verse 26 of the fourth lesson as "synnes of my waxinge age"; the same principle seems to be operating in the translation of "furor tuus" in verse 13 of the sixth lesson as "þi greet veniaunce."

An especially noteworthy example of this tendency to tone down Job's most rebellious remarks comes at the end of lesson seven, verse 15, which in the Vulgate reads: "Ubi est ergo nunc praestolatio mea? Et patientiam meam quis considerat?" The addition in the office of "my lord god, þou it ert!" which has no basis in the Vulgate, works very effectively to turn Job's desperate rhetorical questions into hopeful declarations of faith.

Still, here and elsewhere in the Office of the Dead enough of the original Job comes through so that its complex intentions are not altogether lost. In the seventh lesson, for example, Job's complaint is unmistakable: "y have not synned"—despite the confession in other passages that he *had* sinned. Overall, the movement in the lessons is one of oscillation from repentance to protest and back to repentance. As the compilers of the office intended, the lessons elicit that movement from grief to resignation to repentance and, finally, to hope which those who recite the office are meant to experience. Thus, the response and versicle following the grim second and eighth lessons prayerfully mention Lazarus, who was raised from the dead. Despair gives way to hope. This is the rhythm maintained right through the last of the nine lessons, Job 10:18-22, which dwells on death and darkness, only to be followed by the hopeful Canticle of the Last Judgment.

Surprisingly, the compilers of the office passed over Job 1:20-21, in which Job's response to the death of his loved ones and to the loss of all his wealth is total resignation. These are the very lines one might expect to find in the Office of the Dead, instead of the more vexed and ambiguous laments of the nine lessons. It seems, however, that in choosing scriptural passages the compilers of this office showed a kind of subtlety and psychological insight that entailed letting the obvious go. On the other hand, verses 25-27 of Job 19, which appear not only in lesson eight but also in the response and versicle to lesson one, are ideally suited to an unambiguous consolatory function in a memorial office. These verses were traditionally regarded as a clear Old Testament prophecy of resurrection and redemption through Christ.

But the other passages from Job remain less tractable, even though a few changes of wording and the omission of contiguous verses helped ease them out of the Book of Job and into their liturgical setting. These passages provided medieval worshipers with relatively unmediated access to the Book of Job in its most characteristic mood. Of course the very fact of their inclusion in the solemn Office of the Dead worked a sea change on their tone of rebelliousness: the psalms dispersed between the nine lessons from Job all stress penance and trust in God's justice, and they inevitably color the way we read the verses from Job. Nevertheless, the "little Job," by comparison with the *Testament of Job* or Gregory's *Moralia*, offers a virtually unexpurgated and un-allegorized version of some of Job's most plangent, rebellious speeches. No picture here of Job the saintly host, as in the *Testament of Job*, or Job the patient warrior, as in the *Psychomachia*, or Job the prophet of Christ and the Church, as in the *Moralia*. When medieval writers in the vernacular seem to circumvent post-biblical traditions and turn back to biblical Job, it is to this nucleus of verses from the Office of the Dead that they are very often indebted.

Other parts of the liturgy also contributed to the popularity of Job, though in less striking ways. A small portion of the Book of Job, consisting of selected verses from chapters one to seven, was read in the lessons of the mass for the first two weeks in September. And on November 2, following All Souls' Day, the lessons from Job in the Office of the Dead were read as part of the special office, In Commemoratione Defunctorum.

Another aspect of Job's influence on the liturgy, less formal but no less widespread, was his veneration as the patron saint of sufferers from worms, various skin diseases (especially leprosy), venereal disease, and melancholy, and—somewhat anomalously—as the patron saint of musicians. In medieval Latin and German charms against worms, Job is invoked.[35] As we saw earlier, it was when the Septuagint departed from the Hebrew and added worms to the ample list of his afflictions that Job got his start as a patron of the worm-infested.

Artists in the Middle Ages represented Job's bodily afflictions in diverse ways. There are renderings of Job's worms, scabs, lesions, or ulcers of various sizes, shapes, colors, and distribution (see figs. 2, 3, 6, 10, 13, 16).[36] That Job's restoration to good health is never mentioned in the biblical story did not seem to matter. The cult of Saint Job flourished in the High Middle Ages and grew in the fourteenth, fifteenth, and sixteenth centuries in stride with the ravages of the plague and the spread of syphilis; and in the late-fifteenth and early-sixteenth centuries, when syphilis came to be known as "le mal monsieur saint Job," it reached its peak.[37]

What does Job have to do with music and musicians? Although a number of scholars have tried to explicate it, the motif of Job on his dungheap entertained by musicians whom he rewards with worms or scabs which turn to gold remains something of a puzzle (see figs. 9, 10).[38] We can explain circumstantially how it arose: there are several references to music in the Book of Job itself (21:12, 30:31, 38:3-7), and music is even more prominent in the *Testament of Job*. But the exact motif appears in neither of these works, nor in any early writings on Job I know. Elements of the motif appear in two fifteenth-century vernacular works, the Middle English "Life of Job" and the Middle French *La Pacience de Job*, but in neither of these do we find the same configuration we find in the paintings.

Another source of Job's popularity in the Middle Ages, related to his role in the liturgy and as a patron saint, was the veneration of his various shrines. From the dawn of the Middle Ages, pilgrims to the Near East would regularly visit sites connected with the life of Saint Job.[39] To be sure, not many medieval Europeans would have seen these sites firsthand, but they might well have read or heard about them. All in all, liturgical and sanctoral manifestations of Job must have reached many more people in the Middle Ages than the biblical, apocryphal, or exegetical portraits of Job on which they are based.

3 | The Medieval Literary Heritage

The Early Middle Ages

SIGNIFICANT ALLUSIONS to Job are fairly scarce in the Latin literature of the early Middle Ages.[1] But there are two early references, one in the *Apocalypsis Pauli* (*Apocalypse of Paul*) and the other in Prudentius' *Psychomachia*, both works of great popularity and seminal influence.

Although it was probably first written down in Greek, the oldest and most complete witness to the text of the *Apocalypse* is a fourth-century Latin translation.[2] Like the *Testament of Job*, the *Apocalypse* is a pseudepigraphal work. As the large number of Latin redactions shows, the work enjoyed great popularity despite official condemnations by leading churchmen. Translated into Syriac, Armenian, Coptic, and Slavonic, it continued to exert a deep and lasting influence on the literature of many lands over a period of almost a thousand years.[3]

The *Apocalypse* tells the story of Saint Paul's rapture to "the third heaven" and records what he saw and heard there, including an account of heaven and hell and their inhabitants.[4] One of the saints Paul meets in heaven is Job, first mentioned in passing among those Old Testament worthies who are being rewarded for their hospitality to strangers: "And I saw there Abraham, Isaac, and Jacob, Lot and Job and other saints; and they greeted me. And I asked and said: What is this place, sir? The angel answered and said to me: All those who have given hospitality to strangers, when they come forth from the world, first worship the Lord God and are handed over to Michael and by this route are led into the city, and all the righteous greet them, 'Because you have kept humanity and hospitality for strangers, come, receive an inheritance in the city of our God' " (II, 776-777). The second and more extensive mention of Job places him in the company of Lot and Noah and tells us something more about his present condition and past history:

> I saw coming from a distance another man with a very beautiful face and he was smiling, and his angels were singing hymns; and I said to the angel who was with me: Does each of the righteous have an angel as his companion?
>
> And he said to me: Each of the saints has his own angel who helps him and sings a hymn, and the one does not leave the other. And I said: Who is this, sir? And he said: This is Job. And he approached and greeted me and said: Brother Paul, you have great honour with God and men. For I am Job who suffered much through thirty years from the suppuration of a wound. And at the beginning the sores that came out on (from) my body were like grains of wheat; on the third day, however, they became like an asses foot; and the worms which fell were four fingers long. And the Devil appeared to me for the third time and said to me: Speak a word against the Lord and die. I said to him: If it is the will of God that I continue in affliction all the time I live until I die, I shall not cease to praise the Lord God and shall receive greater reward. For I know that the trials of this world are nothing in comparison to the consolation that comes afterwards. Therefore, Paul, you are blessed, and blessed is the race which has believed through your agency.
>
> (II, 793)

By naming him once with the Patriarchs and Lot and once with Lot and Noah, the author of the *Apocalypse* has apparently followed the tradition according to which Job was regarded as a righteous Gentile living in the patriarchal period—a view of Job that is already present in the Septuagint.[5] But Job's speech, concentrating as it does on the details of his physical suffering, and with its otherworldly orientation, also contains elements of his story that derive from nonbiblical traditions. For example, special attention to Job's worms is not a feature of the biblical story but is paralleled in the *Testament of Job* and in rabbinic and Arabic legends.[6] Here in addition the interest in Job's worms is reinforced by an earlier scene in which sinners who harmed orphans, widows, and the poor—characteristically un-Job-like behavior—are punished by worms consuming their flesh (II, 783). The effect of this anticipation is that when Job describes how he suffered from worms the cruel irony of his trial is heightened and his patient endurance becomes all the more extraordinary.

The thirty-year trial and Satan's three assaults in the *Apocalypse* are not found in the *Testament,* in which Job suffers for forty-eight years and is assailed by Satan in disguise or through Job's wife and Elious some five or six times (21.1a; 6.3a, 16.1, 17.1, 18.1, 20.1, 26.7); nor does the Book of Job specify a thirty-year duration of Job's trial. If we count the destruction of Job's property as one satanic assault and then count the killing of Job's children and his illness as two others, the biblical story can be made to yield the three assaults by Satan to which Job here refers.

It is interesting to note that one of Satan's assaults against Job in the *Apocalypse* consists in urging him to "speak a word against the Lord and die"—words that both the Book of Job and the *Testament* attribute not to Satan but to Job's wife, though in the *Testament* Satan stands behind Job's wife and, as it were, speaks through her. Job's declaration of his intention to remain steadfast—"I shall not cease to praise the Lord . . ."—recalls similar declarations in both the Book of Job and the *Testament.* Yet when Job goes on to intimate that not only did he look forward to an afterlife—a hope already attributed to him in the Septuagint—but that there was a causal nexus between his earthly suffering and his reward in the afterlife, there is little doubt that it is the Job of the *Testament* rather than the biblical Job who speaks. Here we are carried along further in the chronology of the story of Job than in any work heretofore, and for the first time we actually *see* Job enjoying his heavenly reward. Job's closing prayer for Paul and all believing Christians is also the first example of a literary portrait in which Job figures outright as a Christian saint.

There are a few correspondences between earlier versions of the Job story and the *Apocalypse* outside of those in Job's speech that are worth mentioning. In the *Apocalypse* the angels of righteousness wear golden girdles and sing hymns (II, 764, 793); in the *Testament,* when Job's daughters don their girdles, "shimmering so that no man could describe their form, since they are not from earth but are from heaven, flashing with bright sparks like rays of the sun" (46.8), they ascend to heaven, sing angelic hymns, and speak "in the dialect of the Cherubim" (see 48.3, 49.2, and 50.2). Early on in his vision Paul describes a heavenly assembly of angels before the Lord that reminds one of the opening scene in the Book of Job: "Therefore at the appointed hour all the angels, everyone rejoicing, go forth together before God that they may meet to worship at the hour arranged . . . and a voice came forth and said, Whence have you come, our angels, bringing burdens of news?" (II, 762). The angels then report on the activities of men on earth. All of this bears a striking resemblance to the heavenly scene in the prologue to the Book of Job. And Paul's description a bit later of how evil spirits are allowed to assault the soul of a righteous man (II, 766) again reminds us of the Book of Job, the archetypal account of righteous suffering at the hands of the Evil One. These details of the plot of the *Apocalypse,* together with its overt references to Job, suggest that the work may be indebted to the biblical and apocryphal traditions of Job in ways that have hitherto been overlooked.

But whether or not this is the case, there can be little doubt that the explicit notice of Job in the *Apocalypse* was a small but significant factor in the subsequent promulgation of the nonbiblical image of Job as a worm-infested, uncomplaining, perfectly patient victim of Satan's malice and an otherworldly Christian saint, ever confident of, and finally rewarded in, the afterlife.

E. K. Rand describes Prudentius as a "Christian Horace as well as a Christian Virgil and Lucretius," and although it may seem extravagant, the remark accurately reflects Prudentius' cultural significance.[7] Because he was one of the most prolific and innovative Christian Latin poets and because his writings were admired and imitated throughout the Middle Ages, his incorporation of the Job legend into the *Psychomachia*—in many ways his most innovative and subsequently his most influential work—is worth looking at in some detail.[8]

One of the ways Prudentius avoided tiresome repetitions in the *Psychomachia,* which recounts an unbroken and potentially tedious string of victories of the virtues over the vices, was by varying the manner in which each virtue defeats its opposing vice to suit the virtue and vice in question. Thus, in the case of Patientia, it is a tactical passivity rather than a bold frontal assault that leads to the overthrow of her rival, Ira:

> inde quieta manet Patientia, fortis ad omnes
> telorum nimbos et non penetrabile durans.
> nec mota est iaculo monstri sine more furentis,
> opperiens propriis perituram viribus Iram.
> (I, 288, lines 128-131)

[So Patience abides undisturbed, bravely facing all the hail of weapons and keeping a front that none can pierce. Standing unmoved by the javelin while the monster that shot it rages in uncontrolled frenzy, she waits for Wrath to perish of her own violence.]

(I, 289)

Ira, in an impotent fit of rage, finally commits suicide and Patientia marches off to lend her support to other virtues, along with her escort, the noble warrior Job:

> . . . nam proximus Iob
> haeserat invictae dura inter bella magistrae
> fronte severus adhuc et multo funere anhelus,
> sed iam clausa truci subridens ulcera vultu,
> perque cicatricum numerum sudata recensens
> millia pugnarum, sua praemia, dedecus hostis.
> illum diva iubet tandem requiescere ab omni
> armorum strepitu, captis et perdita quaeque
> multiplicare opibus, nec iam peritura referre.
> (I, 290, lines 163-171)

[. . . for Job had clung close to the side of his invincible mistress throughout the hard battle, hitherto grave of look and panting from the slaughter of many a foe, but now with a smile on his stern face as he thought of his healed sores and, by the number of his scars, recounted his thousands of hard-won fights, his own glory and his foes' dishonour. Him the heavenly one bids rest at last from all the din of arms and with the riches of his spoils make manifold restitution for all his losses and carry home things that shall no more be lost.]

(I, 291)

Prudentius' use of the Job story has several interesting features. First, this is only the second time in the history of the legend that we see a smiling Job, the first being the portrait of Job in the *Apocalypse*, with which Prudentius may well have been familiar.[9] Second, Prudentius does not make use of the christological-allegorical reading of Job that was already well established at the time he was writing (this is especially noteworthy given the elaborate christological interpretation of the Abraham story that he advances in the preface to the *Psychomachia*); nor does he present Job as a prophet of resurrection or as an exemplum of hope deferred to an afterlife.[10] Instead, Job's dominant attribute according to Prudentius is courage in battle: the *athleticus Dei* and figurative warrior of the *Testament* and exegetical writings has been transformed in the *Psychomachia* into a battle-scarred veteran in a real war, complete with real armor, spears, and spoils to be won. Third, by introducing Job as the escort of Patientia rather than of some other virtue, Prudentius exploits the long-standing tradition of a "Patient Job" that we find in the *Testament*, the *Apocalypse*, and exegetical writings. Finally, though Prudentius takes no account of Job's righteous rebelliousness—a theme that the authors of the *Testament* and the *Apocalypse* and virtually all early exegetical commentators also overlook—he does include in his portrait of Job another frequently neglected detail from the biblical story, namely, Job's material restoration. For, like God in the Book of Job, Patientia bestows upon Job the spoils of battle as restitution for his earlier losses. By concentrating on Job as a warrior, by portraying him as the escort of Patientia, and by concluding with the restoration of his riches, Prudentius vividly renders three key facets of the Job legend (see figs. 17, 18). If these themes appear in literary representations of Job later in the Middle Ages, it was because the image of Job in the *Psychomachia* helped insure their survival.

Because of the deep and pervasive influence of the Bible on Anglo-Saxon culture, it comes as no surprise to find numerous incidental or secondhand references to Job in Old English prose works of religious instruction, including an entire homily on Job by Ælfric.[11] In addition, there are a number of brief but significant allusions to the Book of Job and the Job legend in the writings of Aldhelm and Bede.[12] It is somewhat disappointing, therefore—and it may well be a result of the vagaries of manuscript survival—that there is no single Old English poem extant devoted entirely to the story of Job, even though we do have substantial Old English poems that treat Judith, Daniel, and other biblical figures.

Job figures directly only twice in the small corpus of Old English verse: once in Cynewulf's *Ascension* (lines 633-658) and once in the *Phoenix* (lines 546-575a).[13] And in both of these works, which most likely date from the eighth or ninth century, Job's role is similarly restricted and his appearance brief. In *Ascension* he is invoked as a prophet of Christ's resurrection and ascension and in the *Phoenix* he testifies to the general resurrection of the dead. Furthermore, in both poems Job's testimony can be traced to exegetical treatises which the poets have followed fairly closely.[14]

Nevertheless, there is a good deal of evidence to suggest that the authors of *Ascension* and the *Phoenix* have carefully suited their derived uses of the Job legend to their larger artistic ends. In the case of *Ascension*, for example, Job appears in the very foreground of the central panel in what has been described as a kind of poetic triptych, composed of three poetic panels: Advent, Ascension, and Judgment Day, which make up a unified work that scholars have entitled *Christ*.[15] This so-called triptych interlaces themes of Divine Mystery and Divine Justice, and one might plausibly argue that Job's prophecy, an elaboration of Job 33:7, is a fitting centerpiece for the entire composition, not merely for the "panel" in which it occurs.

Similarly, there seems to be a broader significance to Job's appearance, brief as it is, in the latter half of the *Phoenix*.

This has been partially explicated by a recent editor of the poem, N. F. Blake: "Job is introduced into the poem as the typical example of the suffering Christian on earth. He represents the good men of this earth who despite their suffering (cf. *wræchwil* 527) keep their faith in God and can look forward to future salvation. The phoenix also represents the blessed on earth and thus the phoenix and Job symbolize the same thing. It is fitting therefore that Job's song should echo the phoenix's: note the verbal echo between lines 125-6 and 549-50. Just as the phoenix does not fear death (368-74), so Job and the good men in this world do not fear to die" (pp. 83-84).

But here we must let the matter of artistic rationales for the uses of Job in *Ascension* and the *Phoenix* rest. The point to bear in mind is that the representation of Job in both of these works has very little to do with the biblical or apocryphal Job traditions; it is determined instead by the tradition of exegesis definitively established in Gregory the Great's *Moralia.*

The same holds true for the most substantial appearance of Job in Old English, namely, in Ælfric's prose *Homily on the Book of Job.* This late tenth-century work by the most prolific and most popular of the Anglo-Saxon homilists is really an epitome of the *Moralia.*[16] As in all his vernacular works, Ælfric had one aim in view when he undertook to write about Job: to make accessible to laymen a simple and edifying vernacular version of a classic document in the literature of the Church. By following Gregory, Ælfric was able to offer up a monochromatic portrait of Job as an exemplary figure, a pious, patient saint, and a type of Christ who is attacked by the devil and remains steadfast under his blows.

In all fairness to Ælfric, we must note that he was well aware of the inadequacies and oversimplifications in his account of the Book of Job. No fewer than three of Ælfric's authorial intrusions in his brief narration of the Job story are apologies for his failure to convey the deep mysteries of his subject. The following is typical:

> We sǽdon eow, and gyt secgað, þæ̱t we ne magon ealle ðas race eow be endebrydnysse secgan, for ðan ðe seo bóc is swike micel, and hire digele andgyt is ofer ure mæðe to smeagenne.
>
> (p. 456)

> [We have said to you, and yet say, that we cannot recount to you all this narrative in detail, because the book is very great, and its hidden sense is above our capacity to investigate.]

Although the brevity of the Job homily and its oversimplifications are enough to warrant this and Ælfric's other modest disclaimers, nevertheless, in its brief compass it does manage to treat a substantial part of the Job story. In addition, it is the earliest extended notice of the Book of Job in the English language, and it was also apparently very popular—all of which lends it a significance beyond its otherwise limited intrinsic merits.[17]

Other Old English works whose indebtedness to the Job legend has been asserted include the *Body and Soul* poems, the *Riming Poem,* and—the most recent addition to the list —*Beowulf.* It was B. P. Kurtz who in 1929 suggested that the *memento mori* in *Body and Soul* had a Hebraic source, and, more specifically, that *Body and Soul* and its numerous Old and Middle English variant versions were ultimately derived from the Book of Job.[18] Over a century ago, the English scholar Benjamin Thorpe had this to say of the technically innovative *Riming Poem:* "The conjectures formed with regard to its subject have been manifold; and it was only recently that the present editor, having taken up the poem in the almost hapless attempt at illustration, was struck by its resemblance to some parts of Job; when on reading over the latter, he soon felt convinced that it was a very free paraphrase from [Job xxix.xxx] . . . all attempts at interpretation by comparison with the Vulgate have proved far from satisfactory. The beginning of the poem corresponds with Job xxix.2"; and though many have demurred from Thorpe's conclusions about the indebtedness of the *Riming Poem* to Job, a number of scholars have agreed.[19] As for the indebtedness of *Beowulf* to the Book of Job and to Gregory's *Moralia,* the case has been made in great detail and with as much conviction as it can possibly carry in Margaret Goldsmith's *The Mode and Meaning of Beowulf.*[20]

In all three of these instances, however, the crucial factor that weighs against the claim of indebtedness to the Book of Job or the *Moralia* is the lack of any clear and overt mention of Job. Explicit or nearly explicit echoes of Job and the *Moralia* may be cited, especially in *Beowulf*, but indisputable allusions of the kind we find in *Ascension*, the *Phoenix*, and Ælfric's homily are absent. Nevertheless, there is clearly a deep thematic affinity between the Book of Job, which Thomas Wolfe described as "the most tragic, sublime, and beautiful expression of loneliness which I have ever read," and much Old English poetry, which, as Northrop Frye put it, "expresses some of the bleakest loneliness in the language."[21] Of course one must resist the temptation to claim indebtedness to the Book of Job on the part of the authors of the *Seafarer*, the *Wanderer*, and other ruminative Old English poems merely on the basis of loose thematic correspondences.[22] For the loneliness and despair of Job were not the aspects of his story of primary interest to the orthodox Christian writers of Anglo-Saxon England—or so the evidence from those Old English works in which some use of the Job legend is beyond doubt leads us tentatively to conclude.

The Later Middle Ages

With the waning of the Middle Ages in the fourteenth and fifteenth centuries, Job's popularity increased. Perhaps this was a result of increased contact between East and West, which provided an avenue for the diffusion in Europe of the Near Eastern pseudepigraphal and oral folk traditions of Job. Or interest in Job may have grown in response to the devastations of war and plague, which led to a sharp increase in the veneration of Saint Job in this period. But whatever the reason, writers in the European vernaculars addressed themselves to the Job legend as never before.

This last statement is true in two senses. For not only was there a dramatic rise in the number of works written about Job, by theologians and poets alike, but there was also a marked shift in the orientation of these writings. It is, after all, a long way from Job, the scarred and silent warrior in Prudentius' *Psychomachia*, or from Job, the prophet of Christ's resurrection and ascension in Cynewulf's *Ascension*, to Job, the lamenting medieval nobleman we meet in fourteenth- and fifteenth-century English and French poetry.[23]

Peter Riga's "Liber Iob," a rimed hexameter poem of 578 lines dating from the second half of the twelfth century, is just one of several French and Latin reworkings of Gregory the Great's *Moralia* to appear around this time.[24] But the fact that it is a part of the *Aurora*, one of the most frequently copied books of the Middle Ages, sets the "Liber Iob" apart from these other works. Soon after its appearance, Peter's *Aurora*—or to use its alternate, more descriptive title, *Biblia versificata*—was adopted as a school text, and it was among the works most frequently cited by Latin lexicographers in search of illustrative quotations. It was employed by poets and rhetoricians well into the fourteenth century, including Chaucer, Gower, and others; and sometime around 1400 it was translated into Old French by Macé de la Charité.[25] Clearly, its potential to influence later writers on Job was very great. In what direction, then, would this influence lead?

About his indebtedness to the *Moralia* and his own modest objectives in the "Liber Iob" Peter is very open:

> Gutture mellito librum Gregorius istum
> Exposuit, per multa notans mysteria Christum.
> Nos merito minimi longeque minus sapientes
> Illud opus sequitur, de multis pauca canentes.
>
> (II, 669, lines 17-20)

[With honey-sweet voice, Gregory expounded this book, through many mysteries finding Christ. I much less capable and far less knowing, follow his work, versifying a few things out of many.]

True to his word, after excerpting and turning into hexameters selected portions of Gregory's exegesis of chapters one to fourteen of the Book of Job, Peter skips, at line 538, to the last chapter, to which he devotes another forty lines. As Beichner remarks: "By comparison with the *Moralia*, the poem is very short; it is an excellent illustration of Peter Riga's remarkable powers of selection, assimilation, and succinct expression" (II, 55).[26]

Yet, as we find on closer examination, in the process of boiling down the *Moralia* Peter worked upon it a change of emphasis that highlighted certain aspects of Gregory's interpretation of Job at the expense of others. Giving only the bare minimum of plot summary, it is the allegorical and moral rather than the literal interpretation of Job that Peter's compressed version of the *Moralia* forces to the surface. Thus Peter persistently draws out Gregory's typological comments, with special stress on Job's role as a type of Christ, as in the following commentary on the first half of Job 1:5, in which Job and Christ are artfully interlaced:

> *Cumque in orbem transissent dies conuiuii, mittebat*
> *Iob et sanctificabat illos consurgensque diluculo*
> *offerebat holocausta pro singulis . . .*
> Dicimus in mundum transire dies epularum
> Cum per discipulos fit in orbe salus animarum.
> Pro pueris Iob sacrificans holocausta parauit
> Cum pro dilectis Christus moriendo rogauit
> Tanquam sanctificat Iob natos quando benigne
> Christus dilectis sacra munera misit in igne.
> Iob sacra mane parat surgens causa puerorum
> Dum Christus surgend illustrat corda suorum,
> Nam de dilectis erroris nocte fugata,
> Illorum tenebras expellit luce beata.
>
> (II, 673, lines 90-102)

[*And when the days of their feasting were gone about, Job sent to them, and sanctified them: and rising up early offered holocausts for every one of them . . .*
We say that the days of feasting in the world have gone when through disciples the preservation of souls has come about on earth. Sacrificing for his sons, Job prepared burnt offerings, as Christ, by dying, interceded for his loved ones. Just as Job sanctified his offspring, so Christ did, generously, when he gave his loved ones sacred gifts in flame [i.e., Pentecost]. Job, rising in the morning, prepared sacrifices on behalf of his children, while Christ, rising, illuminates the hearts of his own, for he dispels the night of his erring loved ones by driving out with beatific light the shadows over them.]

Now when Gregory had expounded this same verse, he did so in three different ways: literally, allegorically, and morally. And to each of these methods of exposition he devoted a separate passage, of which the first and third (that is, the literal and moral) are of about equal length and the second (that is, the allegorical) is by far the shortest. Peter, on the other hand, chose to pass quickly over Gregory's lengthy literal and moral comments—which he treats in four lines preceding and two lines following the passage quoted—so as to fix his attention on Gregory's allegorical interpretation.

We find a similar narrowing of focus in other passages. For example, Peter comments on the opening sentence in Job 10:1 as follows:

> *Tedet animam meam uite mee . . .*
> Tedia presentis uite dilectio celi
> Parturit, ad Christum proclamans corde fideli.
> (II, 692, lines 408-409)

[*My soul is weary of my life . . .*
Weariness of the present life produces love of heaven, summoning the faithful heart to Christ.]

In this case, Gregory's comment, on which Peter's is based, was at least comparably brief, and so Peter did not have the usual leeway in distilling his source into verse. Here is Gregory:

> *My soul is weary of my life.*
> Now whensoever the present life has once begun to grow tasteless, and the love of the Creator to become sweet, the soul inflames itself against self, that it may accuse self for the sins, wherein it formerly vindicated itself, being ignorant of the things above.
> (*Moralia*, I, 544)

Comparing the derived passage with its source, we see that although Peter has not departed from Gregory's interpretation altogether, he has nevertheless refocused it away from "the soul inflamed against itself" and onto Christ. This is the same tendency we find in his interpretation of other passages from the *Moralia*. Peter is consistently moving away from Gregory's "literal" commentary on Job and in the direction of general moral, and more often, christological truths. Another sign of this typological emphasis in the "Liber Iob" is the frequency with which Peter's interpretations deal with the Jews and their rejection by God in favor of the Gentiles. True, this is a feature of the *Moralia* that Peter inherited; but given the relative size of each work, it is remarkable how many of Gregory's hostile comments about the Jews Peter has sifted out and adopted (for example, lines 63-66, 181-188, 189-196, 303-304).

The "Liber Iob" stands at the head of a long list of epitomes of the *Moralia* circulating in the High and Later Middle Ages, and alongside the many picture Bibles which stress Job's prefigurement of Christ (see fig. 13). Together with these, it promulgated the primarily typological reading of Job that persisted throughout the Middle Ages. However, this reading was slowly to give way in the course of the thirteenth and fourteenth centuries to a much more literal reading, in which Job did not cease to be a type of Christ, but became, in addition, an exemplary figure with a reality and history of his own.

Written around the turn of the fifteenth century, and extant in three different versions (two verse, one prose), the Middle English *Pety Iob,* known also as *Lessons of the Dirige,* paraphrases and elaborates upon the nine passages from the Book of Job in the matins of the Office of the Dead.[27] The work survives in numerous manuscripts, and because of its connection with the liturgy, the prose version being found on occasion in the English primer, *Pety Iob* probably ranks as the most widely disseminated of Middle English versions of the Job legend. That the East Midland version of *Pety Iob, Lessons of the Dirige I,* is in three manuscripts inaccurately ascribed to Richard Rolle—all of whose writings had a wide audience in the late fourteenth and early fifteenth centuries and whose Latin *Job* expounds the same passages from the Office of the Dead—served no doubt to enhance its popularity.[28]

The mistaken attribution to Rolle has, for our purposes, a certain heuristic value. For like Rolle, the Job of *Pety Iob* longs for purification and union with Christ and makes no claim to merit any reward or restitution; his only claim is to sincere contrition, confession, and faith in Christ's mercy:

What shal y say for shame and drede,
Or what to do, fool and nys,
Whanne y shal schewe forþ no good dede
By fore so gret iuge and wys?
Al folk on my woln take hede,
Wayte after vertue, and fynde vys.
Say, "God, mercy, þy dome y drede,
ffor in þe, al mercy lys."

Now, crist, of þy mercie we craue,
Haue mercie on vs, and leve noȝt,
We byseche þe, þat come mankynde to saue
To bye vs, þou from heuene vs soȝt,
Oure herytage for vs to haue.
þat wern lorn, þou hast boȝt.
Wyl noȝt dampne in helle kaue,
Thy honde warke þou hast wroȝt.

(p. 118, lines 347-362)

Alongside this portrait of a penitent Job appealing to Christ, in line with Gregory's exegesis of Job, there is in the following stanza from the longer poetic version of *Pety Iob* another exegetical motif:

Putredini dixi, pater meus es; mater mea et soror
mea, vermibus [Job 17:14].
To roten erthe, ryght thus sayde I,
"Thow art my fader of whom I cam,"
And vnto wormes sekurly,
"Thow art my moder, thy son I am;
My systren all ye bene, for why,
None other then ye, forsoth I am."
I shall call hem sustres, lo, for thy,
ffor I shall roote amonge hem.
Of the lowest erthe god made Adam,
of whyche my kynde I had, as he.
Now, lorde, that art lykened to a lambe,
So Parce michi, domine! [Job 7:16].

(p. 137, lines 504a-516)

Comparing himself to Adam and in the same breath appealing to Christ, Job evokes the exegetical commonplace that from early on linked him with Adam and Christ in a triadic figural progression.[29]

Besides Job's figural significance, *Pety Iob* also embraces the biblical theme of Job's request for literary immortality, rendered largely in the anachronistic vocabulary of the medieval scribe:

> Quis michi det vt exarentur in libro stilo ferreo,
> aut plumbi lamina vel celte sculpantur in silice? [Job 19:23-24].
> Who shall graunt me, or I be dede,
> To wryte hem by oon and oone,
> My booke with ynke blak or rede,
> Made with gumme and vermylone?
> Or ellys yet in plate of lede,
> Or grauen in harde flynte of stone,
> That all men, where euer they yede,
> Myght otherwhyle loke theropon?
> I wolde my frendys and my foon
> Ensample take myght by me.
> As thow art thre, and god aloon,
> Now Parce michi, domine!
>
> (p. 139, lines 576a-588)

As the last lines of Job's prayer in this stanza reveal, the poet thought of Job's desire for literary immortality in the frame of Job's exemplary function, much the way Gregory does in the *Moralia.*[30]

In the prose and longer verse texts of *Pety Iob* there is also the postbiblical motif of the Harrowing of Hell. However, in contrast to his testimony in the *Apocalypse of Paul* and the Old English *Ascension,* in which Job is portrayed among the saved, in *Pety Iob* Job's testimony to the Harrowing of Hell is as an appellant, not a beneficiary. It is not until Job utters his last lament that we realize he is speaking to us before his redemption and in great fear of the torments of hell:

> Terram miserie et tenebrarum, vbi vmbra mortis
> et nullus ordo, sed sempiternus horror inhabitans [Job 10:22].
> The londe of myschyef and of derknes,
> Where as dampned soules dwell,
> The londe of woo and of wrechednesse,

Where ben mo peynes than tonge may telle,
The londe of dethe and of duresse,
In whyche noon order may dwelle,
The londe of wepying and of drerynesse,
And stynkyng sorow on to smelle:
Now from that londe that cleped ys helle,
Worthy lord, rescue now thow me,
So that I maye euer with the dwelle
Thorough Parce michi, domine!

(pp. 142-143, lines 672a-684)

In the corresponding prose version of this passage there is an even more perplexing theological complication. Here Job appears to be speaking *after* the Harrowing of Hell, and yet he remains unredeemed:

> Delyuere me, Lord, of þe weyes of helle, þou þat brake þe gatis of bras, and visitist helle, and ȝaf liȝt to hem, þat þei þat weren in peynes myȝten se þee, criynge and seiynge: þou art come, oure aȝeynbier. Delyuere me, Lord, of þe weyes of helle. Reste þei in pees. Amen.
>
> (Day, p. 64, lines 29-34)

A simple solution to the theological dilemma here is that this closing prayer is really the last of the responsories that occur throughout the prose *Pety Iob*. Though ostensibly spoken by Job, the passage is really intended for recitation by the reader —it is his prayer for deliverance from hell, not Job's. And so too with the other laments of Job in all the various versions of *Pety Iob:* though they are based on verses from the Book of Job, they are best thought of as words spoken for a penitent fifteenth-century audience by and through the biblical protagonist. For *Pety Iob* achieves much of its vitality by playing off Job's role as a petitioner against his universal renown as the man whom, in the end, God saw fit to reward (see James 5:11). It is his role as a petitioner who was granted his petition that unites Job with his hopeful fifteenth-century audience, and it is this unity that accounts for his otherwise vexing appeal for redemption from the "weyes of helle" after hell has been liberated.

The freedom with which Job interweaves allusions to the

New Testament and to medieval society is further evidence of his dual function as contemporary petitioner for, and biblical witness of, Christian redemption. As the following passages show, the redemption to which Job aspires in *Pety Iob* has nothing to do with the temporal restitution to which he aspires in the biblical story; on the contrary, his hope in *Pety Iob* is for the only redemption possible according to the orthodox Christian world view:

> But, lord, now lere me with thy lore
> That dedly synne fro me may dryue.
> And Ihesu, for thy woundes fyue,
> As thow becammest man for me,
> When I shall passe oute of lyue,
> Than Parce michi, domine.
>
> (p. 122, lines 43-48)

> My flesshe, the worlde, then ben my fone.
> These ben myn enemyes, lord, echone,
> Euer aboute to perysshe me.
> Lorde, for the loue of Mary and Iohn
> Euer Parce michi, domine!
>
> (p. 131, lines 320-324)

> Y-wys I am nat worthe a bene,
> Of my sylfe, to commendyd be.
> Yet helpe me, Lorde, with thy grace shene,
> And euer Parce michi, domine!
>
> (p. 131, lines 333-336)

These are just several of the renunciatory, self-deprecatory testimonies that Job utters in the course of the longer verse version of *Pety Iob*.

It is in passages like the following, however, even more than in the preceding ones, that Job's identity with the fifteenth-century petitioner is forged:

> Of me men sample take mowen,
> Be ware lest þay folwe my tras.
> I hadde lordship in feld and toun,
> Now on a donghille is my pas.
>
> (p. 109, lines 69-72)

And þou holdest worthy to open thyn ey,
And come to me, and clayme for rent,
To loke on such a wrecche as y,
And lede hym with the to iugement,
þer al mankynde in company,
Atte thy general parlement.

(p. 113, lines 185-190)

Admonitory and penitential statements like these from the shorter verse version of *Pety Iob*, with their anachronistic references to lordship, life in field and town, rent, and parliament, are obviously meant to spur the fifteenth-century reader to repentance with a shock of recognition.

Sometime early in the fifteenth century, an anonymous poet in the North of England set about paraphrasing in verse a number of books in the Old Testament, including the Book of Job.[31] This metrical paraphrase was probably completed very soon after *Pety Iob*, whose influence in places it reflects. Judging by its stanza form, its rime scheme, and its use of alliteration—prosodic features it shares with the York plays—we may fairly confidently assign the entire work to Yorkshire. Recently Severs has judged it "impressive mainly for its magnitude."[32]

Yet our awe in the face of its magnitude—the poem is over eighteen-thousand lines long—is diminished somewhat by the author's forthright admission in the second stanza that the Bible, the Church Fathers, and Peter Comestor's *Historia scholastica* were sources he regularly consulted (lines 13-24). This admission is of less help, however, when it comes to evaluating his treatment of Job. We know that the *Historia scholastica* was not his source, for it neglects to treat the Book of Job, as does the Old French metrical paraphrase of the Old Testament that may have served as an unacknowledged source for other sections of the *Paraphrase*. In addition, the *Paraphrase* has certain features in its portrait of Job that are not found in the Bible. We are thus left with the recently contested assertion that its divergences from the Bible may reflect the influence of an unpublished Old French prose biblical paraphrase.[33]

We may begin very profitably with the first stanza of the poem:

Iob was a full gentyll jew,
of hym is helfull forto here.
ffor whoso his condicions knew
of meknes myȝt fynd maters sere.
Euer in his trewth he was full trew,
os men may in his lyfyng lere.
he lyfed euer als a lele Ebrew,
in þe land of vs he had no pere.
All yf he ware to knaw
full mekyll in erthly myȝt,
In hert he was full law
and dred god day and nyȝt.

(lines 14,089-14,100)

By portraying Job as a Jew and by emphasizing his crowning meekness, the poet at once introduces two nonbiblical motifs. Why he makes Job a Jew, thereby going against biblical and apocryphal tradition (which offer little or nothing to establish Job's religious identity) and against the ecclesiastical tradition (in which Job was generally identified as a Gentile), is a matter for speculation. Perhaps it reflects the influence of Nicholas of Lyra, who, breaking with Gregory the Great and the mainstream of exegesis up to the fourteenth century, decided that Job was not a grandson of Esau but of the seed of Abraham's brother Nahor. Though this genealogy would not necessarily make Job a "loyal Hebrew" any more than his descent from Esau would, it makes a shift of opinion regarding Job's origins somewhat more plausible.[34] A simpler explanation, of course, is that the author of the *Paraphrase*—innocent of any shift in exegetical opinion—assumed on his own that, as an Old Testament hero, Job would have been a Hebrew.

In emphasizing Job's meekness, the poet seems out to stress the exemplary side of his story, even though this entails winking at one of the more profound motifs in the biblical story, namely, righteous rebelliousness. This he was willing to do because of his modest didactic goal, basically akin to Aelfric's some four hundred years earlier: to draw the attention of his audience to the less radical, safely emulable lessons of Job's story. We see a stylistic reflex of this goal in his frequent use of first person plural and indefinite pronouns: "for whoso his condicions knew" (line 14,091); "os men may in his lyfyng lere" (line 14,094); "þe fend þat is our fals enmy" (line 14,137); "All yf our lord wele wyst" (line 14,145); "who wyll take hede may lere" (line 14,196; see also lines 14,290 and 14,390). Also in keeping with his didactic goal, the poet strides over the main theological hurdle in the biblical story: the devil's right to inflict undeserved suffering on a righteous man. On the biblical theme of vindicatory suffering he is silent. Instead, he addresses the problem of the devil's power with the following assertion of divine omniscience:

> All yf our lord wele wyst,
> of all his [the devil's] purpase playn,
> Ner þe lese ȝett als hym lyst
> þe fend þus con he frayn ["ask"].
> (lines 14,145-14,148)

This is followed by an attempt a few lines later to undercut the devil's power further and to limit his right of oppression to the sinful—to set the moral world of Job right-side-up again—by expanding Satan's terse reply to the Lord's question about where he has been (Job 1:7) into the following:

> . . . I haue walked wyd
> ouer all þis werld with outyn wene
> So forto seke on ylka syde
> for syners, and sum haue I sene.
> þor is my bourd to gare þem byd
> tyll I may turment þem with tene.
> (lines 14,151-14,156)

The didactic implications of these words of the devil are clear and purposeful, as if to say: "I am the devil, whose usual business it is to seek out and punish sinners, of whom there are quite a few I bide my time in punishing—so do not be misled by the extraordinary events about which you are now to hear."

As in the Bible, the misfortunes of Job in the *Paraphrase* follow fast upon the heels of the scene in heaven, but the messengers in the Middle English poem, unlike their taciturn Old Testament counterparts, deliver their bad tidings with loquacious verve and, in one case at least, sanctimonious advice (lines 14,197-14,256). This innovation on the part of the English author appears to have no other purpose than the dramatic embellishment and heightening of a scene in the Book of Job that draws its power from its stylized and unembellished quality. Still, the Middle English poet conveys by his embellishments a kind of immediacy and humanity that replaces the timelessness and mythicality of the Book of Job.

Like the biblical story of Job, the *Paraphrase* continues with Job's initially pious response to his misfortunes (lines 14,269-14,288), but not before a major departure from biblical tradition, in which the poet informs us of Job that "fful well he wyst þo werkkes ware / of þe fend and of his fals mene3e" (lines 14,263-14,264). This eliminates the biblical motif of Job's unrelieved ignorance of the source of his suffering, a troublesome feature of the Book of Job that the author of the *Testament of Job* had done away with many centuries before.[35] And as for Job's blasphemous "Let the day perish" speech, it is transmuted in the *Paraphrase* to the following much less blasphemous conditional utterance: "þi mercy, lord, vnto me þou meue, / els may I ban þat I was born" (lines 14,419-14,420).

Later in the *Paraphrase* the poet's main response to righteous suffering is his portrait of Job's faith in resurrection and Judgment Day. Yet despite Job's determined defense, both early and later on in the poem (for example, lines 14,595ff and 14,977ff), of a divine moral order which rests on the settling of accounts in the afterlife, he refuses to accept his comforters' arguments in favor of this order and its operation in his case (lines 14,737-14,760). Instead, as the *Paraphrase* nears its climax Job offers a number of possible explanations for his suffering: perhaps God wished to show his power to sinners by a kind of a fortiori object lesson; or perhaps the object lesson was directed specifically at the three comforters; or perhaps God wished to demonstrate the limits of the devil's power and to expose his treachery (lines 14,845-14,868). But Job soon ceases to speculate and, instead of his bitter peroration in Job 30-31, utters a lengthy prayer of contrition, confession, and praise of God (lines 14,917-15,048).

To this prayer God replies, somewhat incongruously, with an angry denunciation of Job's righteousness (lines 15,073ff), which He declares to have been a mere function of Job's wealth and security—thus conceding a point to the devil!—and He then demands that Job do penance for his sinful response to his ordeal. Obligingly, Job humbles himself even further but stops short of total surrender:

> Lord god, þat gouerns hegh and law,
>   I loue þi sand both lowd and styll.
> My wekydnese now well I knaw
>   þat I haue wroyȝt a gayns þi wyll.
> ffor I haue oft sayd in my saw
>   þat I dyd neuer so mekyll of yll,
> Ne neuer greued a gayns þi law
>   lyke to þe payns ware putt me tyll.
> I wott I haue done wrang;
>   þat sayng rewys me sore.
> lord, mell mercy a mang,
>   I wyll trespas no more.
>
> (lines 15,145-15, 156)

This speech concludes with Job's promise to make amends for his past misdeeds and his prayer for salvation (lines 15,157-15,168), whereupon he is suddenly restored to a state of well-being, his material wealth doubled. That there is no divine rebuke of the three comforters strongly implies, in view of the Lord's unqualifiedly disapproving words to Job, that the poet found their response to Job unobjectionable. It is clear, in any case, that he did not esteem Job's righteous rebelliousness, which God Himself seems at least partially to vindicate in the Book of Job.

To the author of the *Paraphrase*, the paradoxical features of the biblical story of Job were expendable. There is a sense of resignation, a kind of ready surrender before the mysteries of the Book of Job, that pervades the poem. It is strikingly present in the final stanza:

> þus lykyd god forto proue exprese
>   his grett meknes with messelry ["leprosy"];
> And for he fand his fayth ay fresch,
>   he wuns in welth, als is worthy.
> god graunt vs grace to lyfe

in luf and charite,
þat we our gast may gyfe
to myrth. so moyte yt be!
Amen De Iob.

(lines 15,209-15,217)

In order to reach this poignantly simple, if not simplistic, conclusion, the poet had to ignore the agreement between God and the devil to test Job by suffering; he has also had to ignore, among other things, the divine rebuke to the comforters, the speeches of Elihu, and Job's impatient, self-justificatory cries.

But aside from the poem's theological inconsistencies and oversimplifications, there is much of interest in this first lengthy treatment of the Job story in Middle English. As in the *Pety Iob*, one finds in the *Paraphrase* anachronistic details that give the poem a peculiarly "medieval" flavor. For example, both Job and Eliphaz refer to divine judgment as an *assyse*, "session of a court" (lines 14,599, 14,731), and Job refers to his wealth in terms of "ryall rentes with grett ryches" (line 14,283), while the narrator speaks of Job's "ryches and his ryalte, / as robes and rentes and oþer aray, / hys waynys and ploughys and foran fee" (lines 15,181-15,183).

The poet's use of the two Lazarus stories—anachronisms of a different kind—was probably inspired by the reference to Lazarus in the Office of the Dead.[36] In any case the New Testament allusion is applied with particular ingenuity and art in the *Paraphrase*. It comes at what is dramatically the most intense moment in the poem, as Job, alone and in pain, invokes the Lazarus of John 11:1-44 (the brother of Mary and Martha whom Jesus brought back to life) in a prayer of the very ancient formulaic "As thou heardst ———, so mayst thou hear ———"-type:

lord, laȝar þat lay low os [*sic*] led,
  doluen as þe ded suld be dyȝt,
ffull IV days stynkand in þat sted
  and lokyn fro all erthly lyȝt,
þou raysed hym vp to lyf fro ded
  and mad hym man in erthly myght.
So may þou rayse me be þi red

fro dole þat I dre day and nyȝt.
þou wot, and þi wyll wore,
for fro þe is noyȝt hyd,
þat my payns ere wele more
þen yll þat euer I dyd.

(lines 14,977-14,988)

Earlier in the poem Eliphaz compared Job to the merciless rich man who took no pity on the other Lazarus (the poor man who lay at Dives' gate in the parable of Luke 16:19-31); and at that time Job rejected the comparison, turning it instead against his comforters (lines 14,713-14,760). There is real pathos, and great psychological verisimulitude on the part of the poet, in Job's prayerful identification with the Lazarus who was brought back from the dead, rather than with the one who went to his heavenly reward having died poor and covered with sores.

The "Life of Job" is a rime-royal poem that survives in a single manuscript written in "a clear bold hand of the third quarter of the fifteenth century."[37] As one may infer from the following otherwise awkwardly deictic lines, the original function of this text appears to have been to describe accompanying miniatures, now lost, illustrating a unique version of the Job legend: "Here, lo, holy Iob his children doth sanctifie" (line 15); "Lo, here, the envy of this serpent and devyll Sathan" (line 29); "Here immediat begynnyth Iob his persecucion" (line 36; see also lines 55, 113, and 162). If these verses did in fact once point to illustrations, then the author of the "Life," who may have been Lydgate or one of his school, deserves recognition as author of the first extant emblem poem in English. The emblems, however, do not survive, and in their place we find passages from the Vulgate version of the Book of Job written in the right-hand margins of the manuscript opposite corresponding passages in the Middle English text.[38]

To focus attention on these biblical verses would be a mistake, for the "Life" is not a paraphrase of key verses from the Book of Job. Instead, it interweaves the biblical and apocryphal traditions of Job, with additional details that may derive from a lost written source or from oral traditions that may have spread to England with the revival of interest in the Job legend in the fourteenth- and fifteenth-century Europe.[39]

Like the *Pety Iob* and the *Paraphrase*, the "Life," whatever its sources, is consistently didactic. Thus, in the short span of 182 lines, Job's patience is praised no fewer than ten times. But unlike the Middle English works already discussed, the "Life," Severs notes, "concentrates on outward incident and largely ignores the reflective and dialectic content of the Book of Job."[40] At the outset the author follows the Bible in stressing Job's personal piety and wealth, but he soon shifts his attention to Job's excellence as an inculcator of virtue in his children:

> Here, lo, holy Iob his children doth sanctifie,
> And techith his sonnes with-oute presumpcion
> To kepe theire festes, and ever God to magnifie,
> And wysely to lyve with-oute any detraccion.
> And to his doughtres, with-outen pryde or ellacion
> Of their native beaute, he bad them have respect
> Hough bryght Lucyfer for his pryde from heven was deiect.
>
> And by cause in grete festynges is ofte tymes sayn
> Voluptuose fraylte and ydell loquacite,
> This holy Iob for all his children, certeyn,
> Lest they therin shuld synn or offende of symplicite,
> Here offreth to God and prayth unto his deyte
> That his oblacio and holocaust myght habond
> Ayenst theire synnes, if any in them were fownd.
>
> (lines 15-28)

This account of Job's sacrifices for his children after their feasts reflects the Gregorian exegetical notion that these feasts were, potentially at least, unwholesome affairs.[41]

In the passage immediately following, however, the author is back to the biblical story line:

> Lo, here, the envy of this serpent and devyll Sathan,
> Whan he in erthe had ron in his perambulacion,
> God axed him or he had considered His man
> And servant Iob rightfull in lyveyng by demonstracion.

He aunswerd and desired power of persecucion
Of Iob, his possession, and godes, that God did hym sende.
And so He did, but not in Iob his handes to extende.

(lines 29-35)

Here, unlike the *Testament of Job* in which Job is attacked by Satan because he destroyed an idol, Job suffers as a consequence of Satan's unmotivated and malign envy. The passage also portrays the collaboration between God and Satan, a vexing feature of the biblical Job story that we might not expect to find in a brief work whose primary focus is Job's exemplary patience. More in keeping with the poet's didactic aim is his emphasis on the identity between Satan, who in the Book of Job is portrayed as a member of the Lord's heavenly assembly, and the more familiar medieval devil of hell. The point is stressed in lines like the following: "Lo, here, the envy of this serpent and devyll Sathan" (line 29); "This tortouse serpent, oure auncient enemy of hell" (line 43; see also lines 78 and 85).

Other ingredients of the "Life" derive neither from biblical or ecclesiastical tradition but from the apocryphal tradition, be it via the *Testament of Job* or other works no longer extant. Some of these apocryphal motifs include: doctors whose offer of treatment Job refuses (lines 99-105); minstrels who play before Job on his dunghill and whom Job pays with scabs from his body which, when he hands them over, turn to gold (lines 120-124); and comic by-play between Job and his wife about the gold she complains he hid from her and gave to the minstrels (lines 125-133). This last scene is of particular interest because it seems that the author of the "Life" regarded Job's harshness with his querulous wife earlier in the poem—in a scene almost identical to the biblical one in which Job's wife urges him to die and he chides her for her foolish words (lines 92-99)—as his only fault deserving the Lord's rebuke:

Here the blessid Lorde of hevyn, God omnipotent,
Unto his holy man Iob than He apperid,
And sore rebuked hym for that intente
That he to-fore tym had his wyfe cursed,
For whiche of God mercy than mercy he axid

> And of forgevenesse of grete offence
> Of his hasty spekyng and wilfull insolence.
>
> (lines 113-119)

The view that Job's treatment of his wife was improper is espoused in none of the works we have discussed thus far; in fact, the medieval authorities usually praise Job for his tough-minded response to his wife's advice.[42] Why then did the author of the "Life" depart from the traditional antifeminist reading of the interchange between Job and his wife?

One explanation might be that in keeping his focus on Job's paradigmatic patience, the poet singled out the lapse of Job's patience with his wife as a minor offence worthy of divine rebuke. To have addressed Job's impatience with his comforters, let alone his impatience with God, would have entailed theological complications that could easily have impinged on the poet's didactic plan. That Job is rebuked for losing patience with his wife is a kind of a fortiori proof of his perfection.

It is also in keeping with the straightforward didactic plan of the "Life" that its closing stanza narrates the death of Job, draws a closing moral about the transience of all creatures, and points ahead to Job's redemption in the Harrowing of Hell:

> Lo! thus by processe naturall every thyng draweth to ende:
> Dethe sparith no creature of high nor lowe degre.
> Iob, in his senectute, owte of the worlde ded wende,
> His soule with oure fore-faders there to rest and be
> Tyll after the passion of Criste that yt plesid His deyte
> Hym to convey with patriarkes and prophetes all
> Onto the perpetuall ioy and glory eternall. Amen.
>
> (lines 176-182)

Reading this orthodox pendant to the poem, and recalling the emphasis throughout on Job's exemplary patience, we may all too easily forget that in its brief compass the "Life" interlaces several important biblical, apocryphal, and ecclesiastical motifs. It also includes a couple of motifs that are not found in any of the works taken up thus far: the minstrels at the dunghill and the ensuing argument between Job and his wife. These do appear in the Medieval French version of the Job legend that we shall now consider.

La Pacience de Job, an anonymous Middle French mystery play of over seven thousand rimed verses, offers a sprawling but lively and in many ways unique rendition of the story of Job.[43] Surviving in a single manuscript that dates from around 1475, the work went through twelve editions in the period from 1529 to 1625 and we have record of some thirteen performances in the years from 1514 to 1651. Because of its popularity, its stageworthiness, and certain elements of the nonbiblical Job tradition which it alone preserves, it makes a strong claim to being the most significant medieval vernacular composition on the Job theme.

The play opens with a prologue in which we learn that we are about to witness an exemplum ("exemplaire," line 14) of patience and obedience, intended to teach us how to bear our suffering, for suffering is our purgatory on earth and ensures our eternal reward. We are urged to be like Job and endure patiently whatever adversity God sends, trusting that in the end, like Job, we will be rewarded. The speaker of the prologue then submits the play "A la bonne correction / Des clercs qui icy sont presens / La vie des peres lisans" (319-321; "for correction by those clerics here present who are familiar with the lives of the fathers"), and ends with a conventional call for silence and attention—the action is about to begin (1-327).

Two rustics in Job's employ, Gason and Le Villain, quarrel and complain about their lot (328-555). Then, in sharp contrast, Job is shown on his knees at prayer and, a bit later on, at a harmonious family dinner during which each of his seven sons utters a lengthy speech in praise of God (556-954).

Meanwhile, Gason and Le Villain play at chivalry: Gason "knights" Le Villain by beating him repeatedly with a stick, until the latter renounces his ambition to be a knight, having decided that:

> En vray, le dyable y ait part
> En la belle chevalerie!

N'en parlons plus, je te supplye
chascun exierce son mestier.

(1184-1187)

[In truth, let the devil have his share of fair chivalry; let's not speak about it anymore, I beg you, let everyone follow his own calling.]

Now two shepherds, Robin and Morote, come along and drive their sheep into a valley where they meet a shepherd and a laborer who work for Job. The four discuss social justice—or rather the lack of it—and Job's shepherd sums up their grievances in this strikingly communistic speech:

Nous sonmez tous de l'arche Noé
Et cuyde selon mon savoir
Que chascun honme deust avoir
Autant de biens l'ung conme l'aultre,
Et nous en avons si grant faulte.

(1396-1400)

[We all go back to Noah's Ark, and so it seems to me only fair that each man should have as many worldly goods as the next, whereas we have much less than our fair share.]

To which Robin replies with a rebuttal that is encapsulated in the line: "prenons tout en pacience" (1425)—advice with which Job's laborer agrees (1188-1430).

Scenes like these serve to flesh out Job's family life and household along lines that have little to do with the earlier Job tradition. Their purpose is not so much to advance the plot as to comment on social issues of concern to a fifteenth-century French audience. Nevertheless, they also serve to portray in a most vivid, if anachronistic, manner the biblical motif of Job's wealth and piety. Interestingly enough, there is no attempt in these early scenes to illustrate Job's great generosity to the poor.

We now take leave of the rustics, and the scene shifts to a parliament of devils in hell. Satan addresses Lucifer:

Je viens de circuyr tout le monde
Ou tout mal et peché habonde.
Mainctez gens ay fait esbahiz
En passant parmy les pahyz,
Par tous les reaulmes et provinces,
Chez roys, chez ducs et chez princes.

(1435-1440)

Mes oncquez je n'y ay peu veoir
Nul homme ny apparcevoir
Qui ne soient tous entaichés
D'iniquités et de pechéz,
Fors seulement ung fault villain
Ou je n'ay peu mectre ma main,
Lequel Job se fait appeller,
Qui le paÿs veult gouverner.

(1449-1456)

[I come from circling the earth, where all wickedness and sin abound. I have confounded many people while passing through many lands, through all realms and provinces, visiting kings, dukes, and princes . . . But I have never seen or found a person who was not altogether stained with iniquity and sin, except for one false churl on whom I could not lay my hand, who calls himself Job, and would like to be ruler of his land.]

A devil named Berit reassures Lucifer that mankind in general are still wicked and will all be damned. Two other devils, Belzebuth and Levyatam—the latter named after Leviathan in the Book of Job—offer similar reassurances. Each of the devils is then assigned a certain class of sinners as his special prey: Levyatam gets the lecherous; Belzebuth the proud, the envious, and the wrathful, and so on. Finally, Satan gets the assignment of winning Job for the forces of hell, and he takes on Berit as his helper (1431-1698).

The scene now shifts to Paradise, where Satan and Berit seek divine approval of their plan to assault Job. God grants their request, explaining his action as follows:

Pour ce je te donne povayr
Sur tous ses biens affin de voir
L'amour et la parfaicte foy
Certainement qu'il a en moy;

Aussi je veulx essayer
Pour le purger and neptoyer
Conme la precieuse perle.

(1769-1775)

[For this I grant you power over all his possessions; to see the love and perfect faith that he, certainly, has in Me; I also wish to try him so as to purge and purify him like a precious pearl.]

As in the *Testament of Job*, here it is Satan who initiates the testing of Job and God who acquiesces.

Now we are back again with Job's family, where preparations are being made for the dinner at Job's eldest son's house. The invitations are sent. Job graciously demurs but expresses his approval, while his children all very cordially accept (1802-1933).

Meanwhile, Satan is rallying the King of Sabea to make war on Job. Praying to Jupiter, Mars, and his other deities, the king vows to destroy Job and sends his messengers off to summon his knights and counselors to a parliament. At the parliament, the king recounts a vision:

. . . noz dieulx m'ont fait demonstrance
Et m'ont envoyé leur saint ange,
Lequel ne m'a point fait l'estrange,
Qui reluysoit conme soloil.
En verité je me merveil
De la beaulté qui estoit en luy,
Mes je vous jure et certiffy
Qu'il m'a dit les plus grans merveillez
Que j'oy oncques de mes oreilles,
Et m'a dit qu'en la terre d'Hus
A ung faulx villain reclus,
Lequel se fait appeller Job
De la lignee de Jacob,
Et m'a dit en iceste guise
Que ce Job tient la loy Moÿse
Qui est une chose nouvelle
Et ne nous est bonne ny belle
Si sa nacion n'est destruicte
Je tiens la nostre loy pour fricte
Et bien briefment abatue.

(2268-2287)

[. . . our gods revealed themselves to me and sent their holy angel, who did not act the stranger with me, glowing like the sun. In truth, I marvel at how beautiful he was, but I swear to you and assure you that he told me things more marvelous than my ears had ever heard: that in the land of Hus there is a false reclusive churl who calls himself Job, of the line of Jacob; and this apparition also told me that this Job adheres to the law of Moses, something new that bodes us no good. If his nation is not destroyed, our law will be done for, very soon overthrown.]

Unlike the biblical Job or his counterpart in the *Testament of Job,* Job is here represented as a descendant of Jacob and a follower of the Law of Moses. However, elsewhere in the play we learn that Job's kingdom takes in Egypt—a minor detail that links *La Pacience de Job* with the pseudepigraphal *Testament of Job,* in which Job is also portrayed as a king of Egypt (see lines 1947 and 2375, and *Testament* 28.8b).

When the king of the Sabeans finishes recounting his vision, two chevaliers and two counselors withdraw and decide in their private conference that war against Job and the Jews is the proper course. The king sends his messengers to summon his mareschal and soldiery, and when the mareschal, a captain, a marquis, and three armed men arrive, the king once again recounts his vision. The mareschal, captain, and marquis are quick to volunteer. As the captain explains:

Par mahomet, qui m'en croyra,
Nous irons la sans plus d'espace,
Quant les dieulx par leur saincte grace,
Chier sire, le vous ont mandé.

(2522-2525)

[By Mohammed, who may trust in me, we will go there without further delay, for the gods through their holy grace, dear sir, have commanded you that this be done.]

The king sends his soldiers off with a prayer to *Mahon* ("Mohammed"). When they reach Hus, they meet Gason and Le Villain. The mareschal strikes Le Villain dead, and he and his men plunder Job's cattle. On the way back to Sabea, however, they pass the castle of the Chaldeans and there is a great battle, which ends when the Sabeans suggest to the Chaldeans that they join them in plundering the rest of Job's possessions, which they proceed to do (1934-3087).

The Sabean episode, which from beginning to end takes up over two thousand lines, is an elaboration of a single verse in the Book of Job, 1:15. That the names of the Chaldeans derive from several different romances tells us something about the audience of the play.[44] Besides the sheer excitement and suspense, the contemporaneity of these scenes must have been especially pleasing to a fifteenth-century audience. Not all the effects are humorous or light. The death of Le Villain, foreshadowed in his comic "knighting" by Gason in an earlier scene, is a grim, dramatically arresting moment in the action.

After fire from heaven destroys the rest of Job's possessions and all his children, he prays:

> Dieu me doint bonne pacience
> Contre toute adversité!
> Bien voy que toute la plaisance
> Du monde n'est que vanité:
> De grant richesse en pauvreté
> En poy de temps je suis bien cheoist
> Et en tres grant nectessité.
> Le non de Dieu en soit benoist!
>
> (3214-3221)

[May God give me good patience against all adversity! I see very well now that all worldly pleasure is nothing but vanity: I have fallen from great wealth to great poverty, and to great need, in a little space of time. Let the name of God be blessed for it!]

Though in its resigned tone this prayer is superficially quite close to its source, Job 1:21, there are some important differences. Unlike the biblical hero, the hero of the mystery play asks God for patience and renounces earthly wealth. This not only sets him apart from the biblical Job but also connects him directly with the conventionally pious and otherworldly Job in the *Testament*, in the writings of the exegetes, and in Prudentius.

Ironically, Job's wife now utters laments that are modeled on those uttered by her husband in the biblical story. Now that all her possessions are lost, she will have to beg her bread; she would rather die; better never to have been born (3222-3264). But Job urges her to be patient. Hopeful that he will be restored, he adduces the exemplum of Abraham and the binding of Isaac. The colloquy goes on at length, with Job's wife lamenting her losses and Job, without a word of complaint, declaring his patience and praying for God's help in sustaining it and for the forgiveness of his sins (3088-3439). In these scenes, as in the corresponding ones in the *Testament of Job*, the biblical Job's laments for his lost wealth are reassigned to his wife. And lest there be any confusion, Satan now appears and in a monologue confirms Job's steadfastness and contrasts him with Adam, Cain, and Pharaoh (3440-3472).

Meanwhile, the mareschal and his men return to the king of the Sabeans with their booty. He grants them the booty as their reward to divide among themselves. They quarrel. One of the armed men kills the captain, and the mareschal challenges the murderer to a judicial duel. To those who wish to observe the duel the king's messenger gives the following instructions:

> Que nul ne soit si hardi
> De fere signe ne demy
> Ne aussi de soy remuer,
> Toussir ne moucher ny cracher,
> Tant que la jouxte durera.
> S'en preigne garde qui vouldra!
>
> (lines 3806-3811)

[Let no one be so audacious as to make a gesture, or half a gesture, or to shift position, to cough, blow a nose, or spit, so long as the joust lasts. Let he who would take heed!]

After more fanfare and a vivid battle scene, the armed man kills the mareschal. Without a moment's hesitation, the king makes the victor mareschal in the dead man's place (3473-3946).

Besides its topical appeal for a medieval audience, this scene is thematically significant. It portrays crude injustices in the Sabean court that contrast revealingly with Job's trial and vindication in the divine court. The contrast is of course between pagan justice and (anachronistically) Christian justice. And the opposition is dramatically reinforced by the juxtaposition and explicit continuity of Sabean justice and the justice of hell, where the next scene takes us.

Devils prepare to receive the soul of the mareschal. The lost soul laments its idol worship and twice curses the day of its birth (4015-4016, 4111-4112). The devils hang the lost soul in a gibbet and roast it over a fire (3947-4206). By allowing the lost soul to echo the biblical Job's curses, the playwright underscores their very different fates. He further sharpens the contrast in the next scene.

God addresses Satan and boasts of Job's patient response to suffering. Although He allows Satan to go one step further and to strike Job's body, He warns him that Job will prevail:

> Nullement le pourras tempter,
> Car s'il est tousjours pacient,
> Tu te travaillez pour nyant.
> S'il peut sur toy avoir victoire,
> De sa vie sera memoyre
> A jamés, en terre et en ciel.
>
> (4285-4290)

[You will not be able to tempt him at all, for, if he remains patient, all your efforts will be wasted. If he is able to defeat you, his life will be forever remembered, on earth and in heaven.]

This is one of several places in the play that the biblical theme of literary immortality appears, in this case with the further implication that Job will be rewarded in heaven as well. On the other hand, as in the *Testament of Job*, there is no clear idea here or elsewhere in *La Pacience de Job* of two key biblical themes: vindicatory suffering and righteous rebelliousness.

After his interview with God, Satan reports to Lucifer, who warns him that he expects results; if Satan fails to bring Job to hell he will be punished. Now Satan and the other devils attack Job's body (4291-4442).

Job's wife and his servants lament his latest misfortune. But Job himself, after initially praying for relief (4443-4449), praises God and proclaims that his suffering is deserved: "Par mon peché j'ay ceste playe" ("I am suffering this affliction for my sins," line 4500). Robin, Le Pasteur, and Le Messaiger all lament Job's fall in words that recall Job's own in the Book of Job. But Job himself is perfectly patient and uncomplaining, until lines 4595ff, when he begins to utter cries of anguish based on Job 7:16-21, 10:1-9, 10:11-12 (4443-4730). In these speeches, as he quotes verses from the Book of Job that were familiar to a medieval audience from the Office of the Dead, Job drastically reverses his former tone.

Eliphat, Baldach, and Sophar, three friends of Job, decide to pay him a visit, for, as Eliphat puts it: "Au besoing voit on qui est amy" ("In a time of need one learns who are one's friends," line 4754). The friends lament Job's fallen state, while he curses the day of his birth in a speech paraphrasing Job 3:3-8, 11, 24-26. As in the biblical story, Eliphat rebukes Job, and Job replies with an expanded paraphrase of Job 6:2-4. Eliphat urges Job to be patient and thus to win his reward in this world and the world to come. Job's reply is an expanded paraphrase of Job 7:5 and 12:22-28. Baldach also urges patience (5089-5184): God can restore Job's wealth and, if Job is patient, He will. The discourse continues along these lines until after Job's speech paraphrasing Job 19:20-21, 25, 27, at which point Sophar and the other friends courteously take their leave, but not before making a general offer of asistance and apologizing for having stayed too long and for anything they might have said that was amiss. Job thanks them heartily and offers himself as an exemplum of the changeableness of fortune whose life they might reflect upon with profit. When they have left, Job bitterly laments his condition in a monologue that paraphrases Job 10:18-22 (5488-5508); whereupon Satan shouts out his frustration over Job's steadfastness and announces that he will try to defeat Job through a woman, as he defeated Adam (4731-5543).

The scene between Job and his comforters, ending with Satan's surprising and somewhat incongruous shout, is complex. First of all, it develops three important themes from earlier Job tradition: belief in pedagogical suffering, material restitution, and an afterlife. On the other hand, in a break with earlier tradition, Job's comforters are shown to be pious, considerate souls who for the most part do not berate their fallen friend. As for Job, throughout the scene he recites verses from the Book of Job that were familiar to a fifteenth-century French audience from the Office of the Dead; in content these verses are mainly complaining and unresigned, but it seems that their liturgical context rendered them pious almost in spite of themselves. This is probably why the playwright felt no irreconcilable conflict between the speaker of these impatient and unresigned words and the traditionally patient Job he has portrayed thus far. In light of this, Satan's cry of near-defeat is entirely appropriate, for Job's cries are, as it were, liturgically sanctioned. From another point of view, however, this scene is analogous to the very powerful scene in the *Testament of Job* in which Satan the wrestler concedes his defeat, just when Job seems to have reached the lowest point in his trial.

Disguised as a beggar, Satan now approaches Job and laments Job's lost wealth. Job's reply is perfectly uncomplaining: "J'en ay assez, la Dieu mercy!" ("I have enough, thank God for that!" line 5557); and in response to Satan's request for alms, Job hands over some of his worms. Still disguised as a beggar, Satan approaches Job's wife and shows her gold coins which he says he received from Job. She in turn approaches Job and accuses him of holding back some of his remaining wealth. Although he shows her the worms swarming on his body and tells her that *they* are his treasure from God, she continues to berate him, while he continues to pray for God's help. Finally, she abandons him and flees, as a stage direction informs us, to her brother-in-law's house (5544-5714).

These scenes are all reminiscent of the *Testament of Job.* Nevertheless, they differ from the corresponding scenes of that work in many details. For example, Satan also disguises himself in the *Testament* in order to manipulate Job's wife, but there it is as a bread vendor that he entraps her. One major innovation in *La Pacience de Job* is the motif of worms turned to gold, closely paralleled by a scene in the Middle English "Life of Job" in which Job pays minstrels who entertain him with scabs that turn to gold. There is a scene similar to the minstrel scene later on in *La Pacience de Job;* at this point in the play, however, we are left in suspense as to how the worms Satan received from Job were transmuted.

After his wife's departure, Job speaks a monologue in which he questions the justice of his fate. He feels besieged on all sides: "D'une part le dyable me chasse, / L'aultre ma femme me mesnasse" ("On the one hand I am hunted by the devil, / On the other I am menaced by my wife," lines 5718-5719). How can this be happening to someone who has always been patient, always had faith and hope? (5738-5743). God now addresses Job with a series of rhetorical questions and warns him to beware of the devil and his hellish host. Job repents his words. God rebukes Job for complaining and explains the purpose of his trial in terms of the interdependent exemplary suffering and literary immortality themes:

> Je t'ay approuvé, je t'affie,
> Affin que de toy soyt memoyre,
> Conme le fin or que l'on trye,
> Pour donner a tous exemplaire.
>
> (5855-5858)

[I tested you, I assure you, so that you would be remembered—as one tests fine gold—as an example to all mankind.]

The scene ends when God rebukes Job's three comforters and orders them to bring sacrifices, over which they must ask Job to pray.

These scenes are faithful to the biblical story in many details, but there are a few differences worth noting. In the first place, although Job here proclaims the injustice of his fate—as he does throughout the biblical dialogues—there is no subsequent vindication of his rebellious words, as there is in the divine speeches of the biblical version. Instead, after a full and unqualified rebuke, God explains to Job the reasons for his trial—something the biblical hero is never told. The playwright also departed from the biblical story—and from all earlier Job tradition—when he chose to portray Job's comforters as compassionate if conventionally pious friends rather than as self-righteous and inconsiderate counselors.

Then, returning to the biblical narrative, he presents us with the anomaly of the comforters' unearned divine rebuke.

Suddenly, in the next scene, three new characters appear: Patience, Faith, and Hope all agree that Job is worthy of their intercession on his behalf.[45] These virtues approach the divine throne and, asserting that Job remained true to them throughout his trial, request that God restore him. God agrees. He will make Job his *chevalier,* grant him one-hundred and fifty years more to live, and his wife will bear ten children to replace the ones who perished. All this, God explains:

> Pource qu'il me sert en tous temps
> Conme tres loyal combatant
> Et victorieulx champion.
>
> (6229-6231)

[Because he serves me at all times as a very loyal warrior and a victorious champion.]

To accomplish Job's restoration, God sends the angel Michael, who invites along the angels Gabriel and Raphael and the three virtues. All six approach Job singing his praises and declaring that, by defeating Satan, he has won eternal life. Satan flees in defeat as Michael beats him. The virtues present Job gifts. Patience gives him a robe, Faith gives him a braided girdle of gold and silver, and Hope gives him an elegant headgear. And then they lead him back to his house (6084-6460).

Meanwhile, Satan comes before Lucifer to report how he has fared. Satan is forthright: "J'ay esté si bien ramené / Que j'ay laissé sance et merde" ("I received such a good send-off that I left blood and shit behind" lines 6469-6470). Whereupon Lucifer summons the other devils and together they reward Satan for his trouble with another beating. The scene ends with Satan fleeing before Lucifer and vowing to conquer other human beings to make up for having bungled the conquest of Job (6461-6583).

In Satan's frank speech (from which I have quoted only a fragment), as in the actions and speeches of the other devils in this scene, we have a very vivid instance of that "creatural realism" which Auerbach identified as one of the most notable stylistic features of vernacular literature in this period.[46] In this respect, the hell scene is closely related to the scenes at the Sabean court earlier in the play.

This is the last we see of or hear from hell. We now return to Eliphat, who urges his fellow comforters to praise God for healing Job and to join him in telling Job's wife and brother the good news, which they all proceed to do. Job's brother, sister, cousin, and wife each bring him a sheep or a cow and a ring of gold. His wife asks for his forgiveness:

> Monseigneur, je me rens a vous
> En vous suppliant qu'il vous plaise
> Me pardonner de vostre graice
> Si loing de vous me suys tenue.
>
> (6780-6783)

[My lord, I come before you and ask that, if you please, you grant me pardon, by your grace, for having stayed away so long.]

Now Robin, Gason, Le Pasteur, and Le Messaiger—because they have nothing they can give him as gifts—approach Job playing instruments (6860-6972).

In this penultimate scene there are several innovations. The role that the comforters play in the final stages of the action is much more extensive than in other works we have considered. And the conversion of Job's wife is another novelty: in the closing scenes of the biblical story she is not mentioned (even though we are told that Job had ten other children born to him); in the pseudepigraphal and related versions of the story Job's first wife dies and he gets married a second time, usually to Jacob's daughter, Dinah. Except for *La Pacience de Job*, the works we have considered up until now tend to dispose of Job's wife in either one or the other of these ways. Finally, here we find the first clear literary evidence to account for the very popular medieval iconographic motif of Job serenaded on his dunghill by musicians (see figs. 9-11).

In the closing scene of the play Job is back again with his family, once again wealthy, pious, and secure. His brother, sister, and cousin stress the lessons of his story: God sends affliction to purge sin; worldly prosperity comes and goes; those He afflicts He loves. The last word is Job's. He praises God and lists his blessings, for which he asks all present to join him in singing the anthem from the end of matins that brings so many liturgical dramas to a close: "Te deum laudamus" (6973-7095).

There is a great deal more that could be said about *La Pacience de Job.* Its rapid scene changes, sharp conflicts and contrasts, abrupt shifts from high diction to low diction to slang, intricate and varying metrical patterns all merit careful consideration. If they have been neglected in the preceding discussion it is because my purpose has been to consider the place of *La Pacience de Job* among other representations of Job in the Middle Ages and earlier. Even so I have had to be very selective in choosing to discuss points of contact between this play and other works. More than any medieval work we have considered thus far, *La Pacience de Job* combines elements of the biblical, apocryphal, and ecclesiastical traditions of Job with total freedom, not to say reckless abandon. The result is a play that is dramatically vital, if thematically diffuse.

That there is no extant Middle English play of Job, nor any evidence that such a play ever existed, is remarkable. After all, like the stories of Adam and Eve, Cain and Abel, Noah and the flood, Abraham and Isaac, or Moses and the Exodus, the story of Job easily fits the typological scheme according to which Old Testament subjects were treated in medieval English drama: Job's sufferings prefigure Christ's; Job's wife is a fitting companion to Eve and Noah's wife; Job's comforters parallel Christ's tormentors; and so on. Perhaps the indeterminacy of Job's place in sacred history—was he contemporaneous with the patriarchs? with Moses?—is what kept him out of the cycle plays.[47] We cannot be certain. It may simply be another puzzle to be solved by "the-vagaries-of-manuscript-survival" theory. To be sure, in the sixteenth century and after, English plays based on the story of Job abound.[48]

Job's absence from the Middle English cycle plays is made up for by the deep affinities between his story and the morality plays. The story of Job is in fact a prototype of the typical morality play. Like the Book of Job, the English morality plays feature a male protagonist who is at the peak of his physical and material well-being; he comes under attack by agents of Satan (death, the vices, demons, and so on); his erstwhile friends or allies abandon him; in the final moments he repents, appeals to Christ, and is rescued from eternal damnation. In addition to these general and largely implicit affinities between Job and the moralities, there are strong explicit connections in at least two cases: *The Castle of Perseverance* (c. 1400) and *Mankind* (c. 1465).[49]

As medieval plays go, *The Castle of Perseverance* is an elaborate affair, with some thirty-five roles mentioned in the actors' list. It tells the story of an Everyman, a character called Humanum Genus, who is assaulted by the World, the Flesh, and the Devil, succumbs to his assailants, but is finally redeemed through penitence and God's mercy. In rough outline its plot resembles that of the Book of Job. And a paraphrase of lines from Job in the banns of the play makes this resemblance seem more than accidental:

SECUNDUS VEXILLATOR. Þe case of oure comynge ȝou to declare,
Euery man in hymself forsothe he it may fynde:
Whou Mankynde into þis werld born is ful bare
And bare schal beryed be at hys last ende.

(lines 14-17)

Lines 16-17 echo Job 1:21: "Naked came I out of my mother's womb, / And naked shall I return thither."

In addition, in his very first appearance, Humanum Genus evokes the figure of Job in his downcast state:

HUMANUM GENUS. Aftyr oure forme-faderys kende
þis nyth I was of my modyr born.
Fro my modyr I walke, I wende,
Ful feynt and febyl I fare ȝou beforn.
I am nakyd of lym and lende ["loin"]
As Mankynde is schapyn and schorn.
I not wedyr to gon ne to lende ["remain"]
To helpe myself mydday nyn morn.
For schame I stonde and schende ["am confounded"].
I was born þis nyth in blody ble ["condition"]

> And nakyd I am, as ye may se.
> A, Lord God in trinite,
> Whow Mankende is unthende ["feeble"]!
> Whereto I was to þis werld browth
> I ne wot, but to woo and wepynge
> I am born and haue ryth nowth
> To helpe myself in no doynge.
>
> (lines 275-291)

There are no exact quotations, but this speech appears to echo Job 1:21, 7:17, and 14:1.

Though the question must remain moot, it seems likely that substantial reference to Job would also have occurred later on in the *Castle,* in the lost speech of Paciencia. Job appears alongside Patientia in Prudentius' *Psychomachia,* a work with which the author of the *Castle* was apparently familiar.[50] As it happens, however, the only other reference to Job in the play comes in these threatening words of a character called Malus Angelus:

> We schul to hell, bothe to,
> And bey in inferno.
> Nulla est redempcio
> For no kynnys þynge.
>
> (lines 3095-3098)

The Latin quotation is from Job 7:9, where Job broods over his inevitable descent to "she'ol," the Near Eastern netherworld, which the author of the *Castle* has no trouble taking for the medieval Christian hell.

Mankind has been described by D. M. Bevington as "the most indisputably popular play of the fifteenth century."[51] Like *The Castle of Perseverance,* it has a striking, if general, affinity with the Job story: it too shows an Everyman, who is called Mankynde, assaulted by the devil and his agents and saved at the last minute after a perilous struggle. In addition, the visit to Mankynde of Nought, New Gyse, and Nowadays may be meant to parallel the visit to Job of his three trying "comforters."[52] Three explicit references to Job in *Mankind*'s less than a thousand lines make these implicit affinities with Job seem more plausible.

In the first quotation from Job, Mercy expounds the ideal of the *miles christi*:

> MERCY. The temptacyon of þe flesch ȝe must resyst lyke a man,
> For þer ys euer a batell betwyx þe soull and þe body:
> 'Vita hominis est milicia super terram.'
> Oppresse yowr gostly enmy and be Crystys own knyght.
> Be neuer a cowarde ageyn yowr aduersary.
>
> (lines 226-230)

The Latin quotation in line 228 comes from Job 7:1, and mention in line 230 of man's "aduersary" is most likely an allusion to Job's battle with "hasatan," "the adversary" of Job 1 and 2.

Later in the play, Mercy expounds the exemplary significance of Job as follows:

> Be stedefast in condycyon; se ȝe be not varyant.
> Lose not thorow foly þat ys bowte so dere.
> Gode wyll proue yow son; ande yf þat ȝe be constant,
> Of hys blysse perpetuall ȝe xall be partener.
>
> ȝe may not haue yowr intent at yowr fyrst dysyere.
> Se þe grett pacyence of Job in tribulacyon;
> Lyke as þe smyth trieth ern in þe feere,
> So was he triede by Godys vysytacyon.
>
> He was of yowr nature and of yowr fragylyte;
> Folow þe steppys of hym, my own swete son,
> Ande sey as he seyde in yowr trobyll and aduersyte:
> 'Dominus dedit, Dominus abstulit; sicut sibi placuit, ita factum est; nomen Domini benedictum!"
>
> (lines 281-292)

Here the complex biblical Job, the figure of mythical stature, is not the poet's concern. Instead, he portrays Job in monochrome, as a paragon of patience. Although the Bible speaks of Job as "a perfect and an upright man" (1:8), the author of *Mankind* urges his listeners to remember that "He [Job] was of yowr nature and of yowr fragylyte" (line 289). And Job 1:21 is cited in line 292 for all men to emulate. A few lines earlier, in line 287, to obscure Job's larger-than-life biblical stature, the poet actually altered a word in his quotation from Job 23:10. For the Latin "aurum" ("gold") he offered Middle English "ern" ("iron")—so that ordinary men and women will be encouraged to emulate Job, the biblical metal has been debased.

Mankynde's response to Mercy's sermon is extreme. He turns himself into a signboard:

> . . . Her wyll I sytt and tytyll ["write down"] in þis papyr
> The incomparable astat of my promycyon ["promise"].
> Worschypfull souerence, I haue wretyn here
> The gloryuse remembrance of my nobyll condycyon.
>
> To haue remos and memory of mysylff þus wretyn yt ys,
> To defende me from all superstycyus charmys:
> 'Memento, homo, quod cinis es et in cinerem reuertis.'
> Lo, I ber on my bryst þe bagge of myn armys.
>
> (lines 315-322)

The Latin in line 321 ("Remember, man, that you are dust and will return to dust") is adapted from Job 34:15, a *memento mori* offered as a rebuke to Job by Elihu. When he emblazons these words from the Book of Job on his chest, Mankynde hypostasizes himself into something like the personification of Patience or Memento Mori, and the play threatens to turn into a sermon. Fortunately, New Gyse, Nought, and Nowadays, in their rowdy and bawdy way, quickly bring Mankynde back to life.

There are many places where Chaucer briefly alludes to Job, and most notably to those verses from the Book of Job made popular by the Office of the Dead.[53] In a few places, however, Chaucer's use of Job is more than casual, and in light of what contemporary vernacular writers do with the story, especially interesting. The skeptical attitude toward Job of Chaucer's Clerk offers an interesting contrast to the attitude of the morality plays:

> Men speke of Job, and moost for his humblesse,
> As clerkes, whan hem list, konne wel endite,
> Namely of men, but as in soothfastnesse,
> Though clerkes preise wommen but a lite,

> Ther kan no man in humblesse hym acquite
> As womman kan, ne kan been half so trewe
> As wommen been, but it be falle of newe.
>
> (E 932-938)

The irony here is heavy and near the surface. Since it was Job's wife who urged him to "curse God and die," the Clerk's derogation of Job's humility as compared to any woman's is hard to take seriously. Especially when the Clerk makes his claim in a statement of the "all-clerks-are-liars" variety. Yet the Clerk's remark may also convey some recognition of the rebellious and impatient side of Job that most medieval writers overlooked.

A reference to Job a few lines earlier in the *Clerk's Tale* lends this reading further support:

> Hir fader, that this tidynge herde anoon,
> Curseth the day and tyme that Nature
> Shoop hym to been a lyves creature.
>
> (E 901-903)

These lines describe how the father of Griselde reacted to his daughter's suffering. In particular, lines 902-903 almost certainly echo Job 3:1, a desperate curse which Job utters, and which medieval theologians sought to explain away.[54] When Griselde's short-sighted father takes this verse literally and makes it his own lament, the effect is to raise our esteem for Griselde and, indirectly, to deflate Job's reputation for patience. For earlier Griselde had reacted to her trials by reciting Job 1:21:

> "Naked out of my fadres hous," quod she,
> "I cam, and naked moot I turne agayn."
>
> (E 871-872)

By attributing Job's patient words to Griselde and Job's impatient curse to her father, Chaucer in a sense splits the biblical figure. Griselde becomes a new, more perfect Job.

Promoting a patient wife is a novel use of the Job legend, and one for which Chaucer gets nearly full credit. Of the three references to Job I have cited, only the one in lines 871-

872 is found in Petrarch's *De obedientia ac fide uxoria mythologia,* the source of the *Clerk's Tale.*[55]

Equally novel is the militant use to which Job is put by the Wife of Bath. Here is how she taunts one of her husbands:

> Com neer, my spouse, lat me ba thy cheke!
> Ye sholde been al pacient and meke,
> And han a swete spiced conscience,
> Sith ye so preche of Jobes pacience.
> Suffreth alwey, syn ye so wel kan preche.
>
> (D 433-437)

This passage and the lengthier one from the *Clerk's Tale* cited earlier are the first indications anywhere in the Middle Ages of a comic view of Job—or, at the very least, a comic application of his story. As in so many other respects, in his use of the Job legend Chaucer proves exceptional.

There are many works from the Middle Ages which do not refer to Job explicitly but are nevertheless indebted to some facet of the legend. An awareness of the various manifestations of Job in medieval culture puts us in a better position to appreciate works like Chaucer's *Man of Law's Tale,* Gower's *Tale of Constance,* and romances like *Sir Isumbras, Robert of Cisyle, Amis and Amiloun,* as well as other stories of the Eustace-Constance-Griselda type—that is, stories of suffering, loss, trial, and reward at the hands of a merciful God.[56]

Conclusion

ONE WAY TO ACCOUNT for the many different images of Job in the Middle Ages is to look back to the Book of Job. It is a multifaceted and paradoxical work that for thousands of years has drawn careful scrutiny, conflicting interpretation, paraphrase, elaboration—and automatic unanimous praise. To its would-be imitators, however, it always presented, and still presents, hazards as well as riches. To some extent these are the same hazards that any author adapting any classic must face. As Johnson wrote: "We have been too early acquainted with the poetical heroes to expect any pleasure from their revival; to show them as they already have been shown, is to disgust by repetition; to give them new qualities or new adventures, is to offend by violating received notions."[1] How could the story of Job be retold so as not to "disgust by repetition" or "offend by violating received notions"?

The dilemma is real but not insoluble. There are many character adaptations—Chaucer's Troilus, Shakespear's Caesar, Milton's Adam and Eve, and Tennyson's Arthur are but a few that come to mind immediately—in which the violation of received notions is anything but offensive. On the contrary, these violations of received notions soon become, for succeeding generations, the standard against which newer adaptations of a classic theme will be judged. In short, they become received notions in their own right. And this is exactly what happened with Job in the Middle Ages: apocryphal and ecclesiastical adaptations of his legend were the received notions that largely displaced the biblical tradition.

In our time the situation is very different. Works like the *Testament of Job*, *Pety Iob*, *La Pacience de Job*, or even more recent works, such as Blake's *Job* or MacLeish's *J. B.*, may achieve a certain vigor and independent life, but they fail to cast a shadow over the biblical story.[2] The Book of Job is the liminal work in the history of the Job legend. All imaginative works that treat Job in a more than cursory way are in dialogue with the Book of Job. The Book of Job is thus not only a point of departure in a history of the Job legend but also, in a sense, the goal—the work that all subsequent works on Job have sought to interpret, revise, or refute.

To take hold of the Book of Job, says St. Jerome, is to take hold of a work as elusive as an eel: "si velis anguillam, vel muraenulam strictis tenere manibus, quanto fortius presseris, tanto citius elabitur" ("if you should wish to close your hand and hold on to an eel or a lamprey, the harder you press the quicker it will escape").[3] Unlike most postbiblical works about Job, the Book of Job abides its contraries without any irritable reaching after unitary resolutions. It refuses to declare in favor of a Job who is altogether rebellious or altogether submissive, always wealthy or always impoverished. Instead the Book of Job allows the tensions of a now satisfied, now suffering, now rebellious, and now submissive Job to stand, unresolved. And that may be the key to its durability.

1. *Bible, c. 1238. Half-figures of Job, nimbed, holding an open roll inscribed with Job 2:10 and his wife holding an open roll inscribed with Job 2:9 (adapted from an entry in the Princeton Index of Christian Art, hereafter referred to as PICA).*

2. *Bible, c. 1240. Job's wife holding an open roll and his three comforters and Elihu (?) wearing conical hats, all standing beside Job seated on a dungheap holding an open roll in his left hand (PICA).*

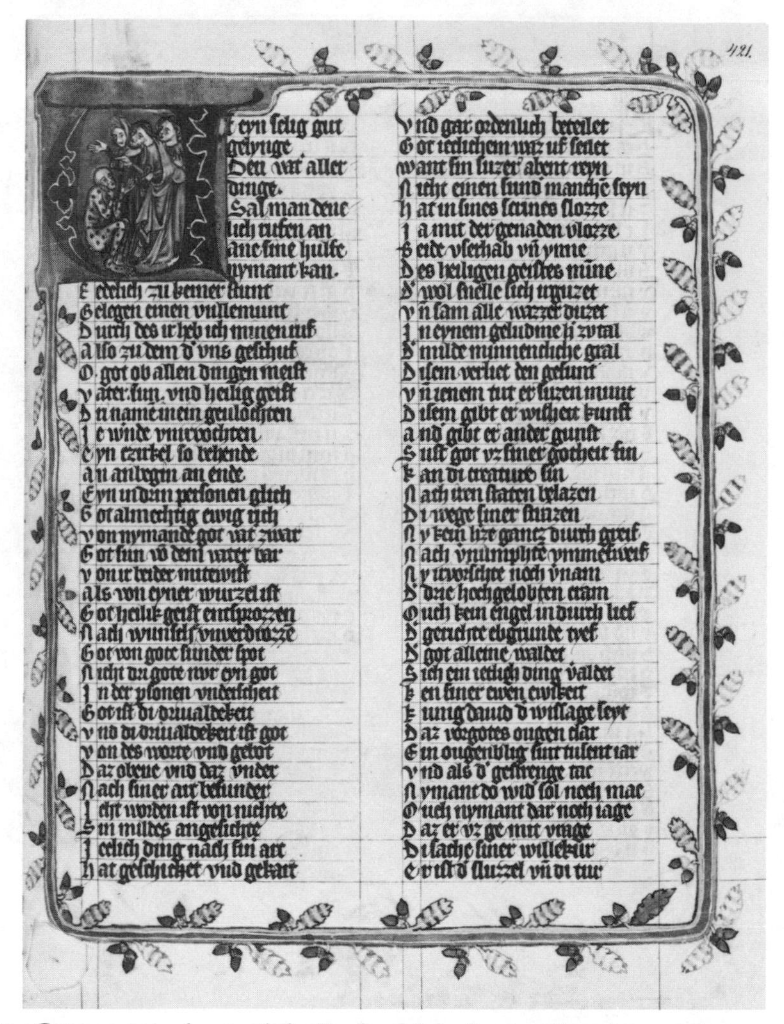

3. *German paraphrase of the Book of Job, fourteenth century. Job on a dungheap, covered with spots and suffering from baldness. His wife and two comforters stand opposite.*

4. *Bible, twelfth century. Job's seven sons and three daughters behind Job, who kneels, his hands extended toward God. Below: Job seated on a dung-heap, his wife standing opposite holding an open roll* (*PICA*).

5. *Chartres Cathedral, c. 1255. A conflation of several scenes from the Book of Job: God and two angels look on as Satan strikes Job "from head to foot"; three comforters approach from the left; and Job's wife looks on from the right, close enough so that Job's free foot touches her robe.*

6. *Notre Dame de Paris, early thirteenth century. Job, seated on a dung-heap is visited by three very downcast comforters and his wife, who seems almost to be bearing up the comforter on the far right.*

7. *Greek Bible, c. 900. Job on a dungheap naked and covered with sores, his wife offering food at the end of a stick, while covering her mouth and nose with a fold of her robe; three royal comforters approach accompanied by a press of soldiers.*

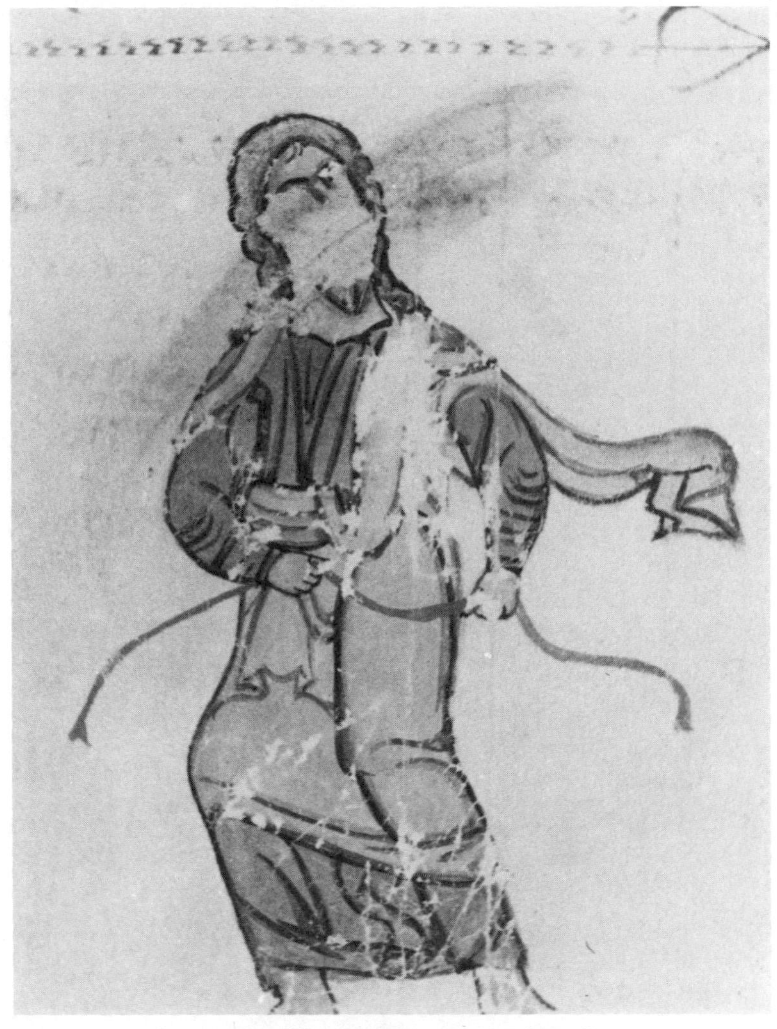

8. *Greek Bible, eighth century. Job "girding his loins."*

9. *Altarpiece, c. 1480-1483. Cycle of scenes from the nonbiblical life of Job, including visit of an angel (upper left) and Job and the minstrels (lower right).*

10. *Pierre de Nesson's* Neuf leçons de Job, *fifteenth century. Job, seated on a large dungheap, offers a coin to minstrels who entertain him.*

11. *Albrecht Dürer, Jabach altarpiece, 1503-1504. Job seated on a dung-heap; his wife empties a bucket over him while musicians entertain him. In the distance, flames and a solitary figure in flight toward Job.*

12. *Floreffe Bible, c. 1155. Pictorial exegesis of the Book of Job. Top: Job kneels beside a burnt offering and prays for his children. Above the central design: Job's seven sons and three daughters. Below the central design: the Twelve Apostles. In the seven medallions of the central rose: the seven virtues produced by the gifts of the Holy Ghost. In the eighth and lowest medallion: the right hand of God emanating rays onto the apostles. In the center: Faith, Charity, and Hope. Below the central design: Christ pleads with his Father on the apostles' behalf. Bottom: David and Paul, representing Old and New Covenants; scenes of Job and his wife. (Except with respect to the last scene, this analysis follows Katzenellenbogen, pp. 37-38.)*

13. Le Miroir de l'humaine salvation, *fifteenth century. Right: Job seated on a dungheap flanked by his wife and Satan. Superscription reads: "Satan beat him with whips and his wife beat him with words" (cp. Gregory the Great,* Moralia, *I, 139). Left: Lamech is beaten by his wives (see Gen. 4:19-24). In various manuscripts of the* Biblia pauperum, *as here, Lamech's suffering is paired with Job's, and both are presented flanking the Flagellation of Christ (see Réau, II, part 1, 316-317).*

14. Liber Floridus, *twelfth century. Horned devil astride horned, ox-like Behemoth.*

15. Liber Floridus, *twelfth century. Antichrist seated on the coiling tail of a dragon-like Leviathan swimming in the sea.*

16. *German woodcut, c. 1490. Saint Job, covered with sores (leprosy?), flanked by male and female petitioners, who are also covered with sores. Above Job's head is a scroll with the motto: "O thou holy Saint Job." From the upper right the hand of God extends toward Job in benediction.*

17. *Prudentius,* Psychomachia, *ninth century. Helmeted Patience leads Job by the hand through the battle line.*

18. *Prudentius,* Psychomachia, *ninth century. Patience and Job, with cane, seated outside fortified building and above the battle.*

Bibliography
Notes
Index

Abbreviations

AB	*The Art Bulletin*
AJSLL	*American Journal of Semitic Languages and Literatures*
ANCL	*Ante-Nicene Christian Library*
BT	*Babylonian Talmud*
EETS	Early English Text Society
HUCA	*Hebrew Union College Annual*
JBL	*Journal of Biblical Literature*
JWCI	*Journal of the Warburg and Courtauld Institutes*
MGH	*Monumenta Germaniae Historica*
MLA	Modern Language Association of America
PL	*Patrologia Latina*
RTAM	*Recherches de théologie ancienne et médiévale*
SBL	Society of Biblical Literature
SLNPNF	*Select Library of Nicene and Post-Nicene Fathers*
SPCK	Society for Promoting Christian Knowledge
SVT	Supplements to *Vetus Testamentum*
VT	*Vetus Testamentum*
ZAW	*Zeitschrift für die alttestamentliche Wissenschaft*

Bibliography

Primary Sources

Ælfric. *The Homilies of the Anglo-Saxon Church: The First Part Containing the Sermones Catholici or Homilies of Ælfric.* Trans. and ed. Benjamin Thorpe. 2 vols. London: Printed for the Aelfric Society, 1844-1846.

———. *Homilies of Aelfric: A Supplementary Collection.* Ed. John C. Pope. 2 vols. EETS, 259, 260. London: Oxford University Press, 1967, 1968.

Analecta Anglo-Saxonica. Ed. Benjamin Thorpe. London: Smith, Elder & Co., 1846.

Ante-Nicene Christian Library: Translations of the Writings of the Fathers down to A.D. 325. Ed. Alexander Roberts and James Donaldson. 24 vols. Edinburgh, 1867-1872.

Apocalypse of Paul. In *New Testament Apocrypha,* II, 755-798. Ed. Edgar Hennecke and W. Schneemelcher; English translation ed. R. M. Wilson. 2 vols. London: Lutterworth Press, and Philadelphia: The Westminster Press, 1963, 1965.

Babylonian Talmud, The. Trans. and ed. Isidore Epstein. 18 vols. London: Soncino Press, 1935-1952 (rpt. 1961).

Bede. *Venerabilis Baedae historiam ecclesiasticam gentis Anglorum, historiam abbatum, epistolam ad Ecgberctum una cum historia abbatum auctore anonymo . . .* Ed. Charles Plummer. 2 vols. Oxford: Clarendon Press, 1896.

Bible. [Douay Version: Old Testament, 1609; New Testament, 1582.] *The Holy Bible Translated from the Latin Vulgate Diligently Compared with the Hebrew, Greek, and Other Editions in Divers Languages.* New York: Edward Dunigan, 1844.

———. [Job. Hebrew Masoretic text.] *Mikraot Gedolot,* X. New York: Pardes, 1951.

———·*Job: A New Translation with Introduction and Commentary.* Trans. and ed. Marvin H. Pope. 3rd ed. The Anchor Bible, 15. Garden City, N.Y.: Doubleday & Co., 1973.

———· [King James Version, 1611.] *The Holy Bible Containing the Old and New Testaments Translated out of the Original Tongues and with the Former Translations Diligently Compared and Revised.* Cleveland and New York: The World Publishing Co., n.d.

———· *The New English Bible: The Old Testament, the New Testament, the Apocrypha.* 3 vols. Cambridge: Oxford University Press and Cambridge University Press, 1970, 1961, 1970.

———· *The Septuagint Bible in the Translation of Charles Thomson, Secretary of the Continental Congress of the United States of America, 1744-1789.* Rev. edition by C. A. Muses. Colorado: The Falcon's Wing Press, 1954.

———· [Vulgate.] *Biblia Sacra iuxta Vulgatam Clementinam nova editio.* Madrid: Biblioteca de Autores Cristianos, 1965.

———· [Wycliffite Bible.] *The Holy Bible Containing the Old and New Testaments, with the Apocryphal Books in the Earliest English Versions Made from the Latin Vulgate by John Wycliffe and His Followers.* Ed. Josiah Forshall and Frederic Madden. 4 vols. Oxford: Oxford University Press, 1850.

Breviarium ad usum insignis ecclesiae Sarum. Ed. Francis Procter and Christopher Wordsworth. 3 vols. Cambridge: Cambridge University Press, 1879-1886 (rpt. Gregg International Publishers, 1970).

Chaucer, Geoffrey. *The Complete Works of Geoffrey Chaucer.* Ed. Walter W. Skeat. 6 vols. and supplement. Oxford: Clarendon Press, 1894-1897.

———· *The Works of Geoffrey Chaucer.* Ed. F. N. Robinson. 2nd ed. Boston: Houghton Mifflin Co., 1957.

Corpus Christianorum: Series Latina. Belgium: Turnhout, 1953- .

Early English Homilies from the Twelfth Century MS. Vesp. D. XIV. Ed. Rubie D. Warner. EETS, o.s. 152. London: Kegan Paul, 1917 (for 1915).

[Egeria.] *Ethérie: Journal de Voyage.* Trans. and ed. Hélène Pétré. Sources Chrétiennes, 21. Paris: Editions du Cerf, 1948.

The Exeter Book. Ed. George Philip Krapp and E. V. K. Dobbie. The Anglo-Saxon Poetic Records, 3. New York: Columbia University Press, 1936 (rpt. 1966).

Fourteenth Century Verse and Prose. Ed. Kenneth Sisam. Oxford: Clarendon Press, 1921 (rpt. 1970).

Gregory the Great. *Morals on the Book of Job.* Ed. Charles Marriott and trans. anon. 4 parts in 3 vols. Oxford: J. H. Parker, 1848-1850.

Histoire de notre seigneur Job. In Haim Zafrani, "Une histoire de Job en Judéo-Arabe du Maroc." *Revue des études islamiques,* 36 (1968), 279-315.

L'Hystore Job: An Old French Verse Adaptation of Compendium In Iob *by Peter of Blois,* I: *Texts.* Ed. Joseph Gildea, O.S.A. Villanova, Penn.: St. Thomas Press, 1974.

Job. See Bible.

Julian the Arian. *Der Hiobkommentar des Arianers Julian.* Ed. Dieter Hagedorn. Patristische Texte und Studien, 14. Berlin and New York: de Gruyter, 1973.

Koran. *The Koran Interpreted.* Trans. and ed. Arthur J. Arberry. London: Oxford University Press, 1964.

La Tour-Landry. *The Book of the Knight of La Tour Landry.* Ed. Thomas Wright. Rev. ed. EETS, o.s. 33. London: Kegan Paul, 1906.

Le Livre de Job, version Copte Bohäirique, pp. 213-339. Trans. and ed. Abbé E. Porcher. *Patrologia Orientalis,* 18. Paris: Firmin-Didot, 1924.

Macé de la Charité. *La Bible de Macé de la Charité: Ruth, Judith, Tobie, Esther, Daniel, Job.* Ed. Henri C.-M. van der Krabben. Leiden: Universitaire Pers, 1964.

The Macro Plays: The Castle of Perseverance, Wisdom, Mankind. Ed. Mark Eccles. EETS, o.s. 262. London: Oxford University Press, 1969.

Maimonides, Moses. *The Guide for the Perplexed.* Trans. M. Friedländer. 2nd ed. New York: Dover, 1956.

"A Middle English Metrical Life of Job." Ed. G. N. Garmonsway and R. R. Raymo. In *Early English and Norse Studies Presented to Hugh Smith in Honour of his Sixtieth Birthday,* pp. 77-98. Ed. Arthur Brown and Peter Foote. London: Methuen, 1963.

A Middle English Metrical Paraphrase of the Old Testament. Ed. Herbert Kalén and Urban Ohlander. *Göteborgs Högskolas Årsskrift,* 28 (1922), I-CXCV and 1-176; *Göteborgs Universitets Årsskrift,* 61, no. 2 (1955); *Göteborgs Universitets Årsskrift,* 66, no. 7 (1960); *Gothenburg Studies in English,* 16 (1963).

Le Mistère du Viel Testament, V, 1-51. Ed. James de Rothschild. 6 vols. Société des anciens textes français. Paris: Firmin-Didot, 1878-1891.

Monumenta Germaniae Historica: Auctorum antiquissimorum. 15 vols. Berlin: Weidmann, 1887-1919.

Monumenta Germaniae Historica: Poetarum Latinorum Medii Aevi. 4 vols. Berlin: Weidmann, 1881-1896.

Nicholas of Lyra. *Biblia Latina cum Postillis Nicolai de Lyra,* II, hh4. 4 vols. Venice, 1489.

The Oxford Book of Carols. Ed. Percy Dearmer, R. Vaughan Williams, and Martin Shaw. London: Oxford University Press, 1928.

La Pacience de Job: Mystère anonyme du XVe siècle (ms. fr. 1774). Ed. Albert Meiller. Paris: Klincksieck, 1971.

Paraphrase. See *A Middle English Metrical Paraphrase of the Old Testament.*

Patrologia Latina. Ed. J. P. Migne. 221 vols. Paris, 1844-1864.

Peter of Blois. *Compendium in Iob.* See *L'Hystore Job.*

Peter Riga. *Aurora Petri Rigae Biblia Versificata: A Verse Commentary on the Bible.* Ed. Paul E. Beichner. 2 vols. Publications in Mediaeval Studies: The University of Notre Dame, 19. Notre Dame, Ind.: University of Notre Dame Press, 1965.

The Phoenix. Ed. N. F. Blake. Old and Middle English Texts. Manchester, England: Manchester University Press, and New York: Barnes and Noble, 1964.

Pierre de Nesson. *Pierre de Nesson et ses oeuvres.* Ed. Arthur Piaget and Eugenie Droz. Paris: Droz, 1925.

Prudentius. *Prudence: Psychomachie.* Trans. and ed. Maurice Lavarenne. Paris: Société Française d'Imprimerie et de Librairie, 1933.

———. *Prudentius* [Works]. Trans and ed. H. J. Thompson. 2 vols. Loeb Classical Library. Cambridge: Harvard University Press, and London: Heinemann, 1949 (rpt. 1962).

The Prymer or Lay Folks' Prayer Book. Ed. Henry Littlehales. 2 vols. EETS, o.s. 105, 109. London: Kegan Paul, 1895 (rpt. as one vol., Kraus, 1973).

Pseudo-Philo. *Pseudo-Philo's Liber antiquitatum biblicarum.* Ed. Guido Kisch. Publications in Mediaeval Studies: The University of Notre Dame, 10. Notre Dame, Ind.: University of Notre Dame Press, 1949.

A Select Library of Nicene and Post-Nicene Fathers of the Christian Church. 2nd ser. Trans. and ed. Philip Schaff and Henry Wace. 14 vols. New York: The Christian Literature Co., 1890-1900.

Le Testament de Job: Introduction, traduction, et notes. Trans. and ed. Marc Philonenko. *Semitica: Cahiers publiés par l'Institut d'études sémitiques de l'Université de Paris,* 18 (1968).

Testament of Job, pp. lxxii-cii, 103-137. Ed. Montague Rhodes James. In *Texts and Studies: Contributions to Biblical and Patristic Literature,* vol. V, part 1: *Apocrypha Anecdota.* 2nd ser. Ed. J. Armitage Robinson. Cambridge: Cambridge University Press, 1897.

The Testament of Job. Ed. Robert A. Kraft et al. SBL, Texts and Translations, 5; Pseudepigrapha Series, 4. Missoula, Mont.: SBL and Scholars' Press, 1974.

"*The Testament of Job,* an Essene Midrash on the Book of Job." Trans. and ed. Kaufmann Kohler. In *Semitic Studies in Memory of Rev. Dr. Alexander Kohut.* Ed. George Alexander Kohut. Berlin: Calvary, 1897.

"The Testament of Job: Introduction, Translation, and Notes." Trans. and ed. Russell Paul Spittler. Diss. Harvard University, 1971.

Twenty-Six Political and Other Poems (Including 'Petty Job'). Ed. Josef Kail. EETS, o.s. 124. London: Kegan Paul, 1904.

The Vercelli Book. Ed. George Philip Krapp. The Anglo-Saxon Poetic Records, 2. New York: Columbia University Press, 1932 (rpt. 1969).

The Wheatley Manuscript. Ed. Mabel Day. EETS, o.s. 155. London: Oxford University Press, 1921 (for 1917).

Secondary Sources

Albright, William Foxwell. "The Name of Bildad the Shuhite." *AJSLL,* 44 (1927), 31-36.

———. "Some Canaanite-Phoenician Sources of Hebrew Wisdom." *SVT,* 3 (1955), 1-15.

Allen, Hope Emily. *Writings Ascribed to Richard Rolle, Hermit of Hampole, and Materials for his Biography.* MLA Monograph

Series, 3. New York: D. C. Heath, and London: Oxford University Press, 1927.

Allen, Margaret J. "The Book of Job in Middle English Literature (1100-1500)." Diss. University of London, 1970.

Alphandéry, P. "Le Satan du 'Libre de Job' dans le Moyen-Age Latin." *Revue de Paris,* 4 (1930), 875-897.

Alt, A. "Zur Vorgeschichte des Buches Hiob." *ZAW,* 14 (1937), 265-268.

Anderson, George Kunler. "Old English Literature." In *The Medieval Literature of Western Europe: A Review of Research, Mainly 1930-1960,* pp. 37-71. Ed. John H Fisher. New York: New York University Press (for MLA), 1966.

Apt, Naftali. *Die Hiobserzählung in der arabischen Literatur, Erster Teil: Zwei arabische Hiobhandschriften der Kgl. Bibliothek zu Berlin.* Diss. Heidelberg, 1913. Kirchhain: N.-L.: Schmersow, 1913.

Auerbach, Erich. *Mimesis: The Representation of Reality in Western Literature.* Trans. Willard R. Trask. Princeton: Princeton University Press, 1953.

Avni, Abraham. "The Influence of the Bible on American Literature: A Review of Research from 1955 to 1965." *Bulletin of Bibliography,* 27 (1970), 101-106.

———. "The Influence of the Bible on European Literatures: A Review of Research from 1955 to 1965." *Yearbook of Comparative and General Literature,* 19 (1970), 39-57.

Bacher, Wilhelm. "Das Targum zu Hiob." *Monatsschrift für Geschichte und Wissenschaft des Judenthums,* 20 (1871), 208-223.

Baeck, Leo. *This People Israel: The Meaning of Jewish Existence.* Trans. Albert H. Friedlander. London: W. H. Allen, 1965.

Bailey, Terence. *The Processions of Sarum and the Western Church.* Pontifical Institute of Mediaeval Studies, Studies and Texts, 21. Toronto: Pontifical Institute of Mediaeval Studies, 1971.

Bandmann, Günter. *Melancholie und Musik: Ikonographische Studien.* Wissenschaftliche Abhandlungen des Arbeitsgemeinschaft für Forschung des Landes Nordhein-Westfalen, 12. Cologne and Opladen: Westdeutscher Verlag, 1960.

Bardsley, Charles. *Curiosities of Puritan Nomenclature.* London: Chatto and Windus, 1880.

Barton, G. A. "The Composition of Job 24-30." *JBL,* 30 (1911), 67-77.

Baumgärtel, Friedrich. *Der Hiobdialog: Aufriss und Deutung.*

Stuttgart: Kohlhammer, 1933.

Besserman, Lawrence Leon. "The Story of Job: A Survey of Its Literary History, with Special Reference to Medieval English Literature." Diss. Harvard University, 1973.

———. "A Note on the Source of Ælfric's Homily on the Book of Job." *English Language Notes*, 10 (1973), 248-252.

Bič, Miloš. "Le juste et l'impie dans le livre de Job." *SVT*, 15 (1966), 33-43.

Bloomfield, Morton W. *Essays and Explorations: Studies in Ideas, Language, and Literature.* Cambridge: Harvard University Press, 1970.

Bouchard, Charles. "Les Conjectures de J. Rollet sur la maladie de Job jugeés par Bouchard." *Aesculape*, 15 (1925), 105-107.

Bradley, George Granville. *Lectures on the Book of Job.* Oxford: Clarendon Press, 1887.

Brody, Saul Nathaniel. *The Disease of the Soul: Leprosy in Medieval Literature.* Ithaca, N.Y., and London: Cornell University Press, 1974.

Buber, Martin. *The Prophetic Faith.* Trans. Carlyle Witton-Davies. New York: Harper & Row, 1960.

Budde, R. "Job." In *Lexikon der Christlichen Ikonographie.* Ed. Engelbert Kirschbaum, S. J., et al. Rome, Freiburg, Basel, Vienna: Herder, 1970.

Bussler, Erich. "Hiob und Prometheus: Zwei Vorkämpfer der göttlichen Gerechtigkeit, ein Vergleich." In *Sammlung gemeinverständlicher wissenschaftlicher Vorträge*, n.s. Ed. R. Birchow. 12th ser., 265-288. Hamburg: Verlagsanstalt A.-G., 1897.

Buttenweiser, Moses. *The Book of Job.* London: Hodder & Stoughton, 1922.

Catry, Patrick. "Épreuves du juste et mystère de Dieu: Le commentaire litteral du *Livre de Job* par saint Grégoire le Grand." *Revue des études augustiniennes*, 18 (1972), 124-144.

Coleman, Edward D. *The Bible in English Drama: An Annotated List of Plays Including Translations from Other Languages.* New York: New York Public Library, 1931.

Collins, John J. "Structure and Meaning in the Testament of Job." *SBL Seminar Papers*, I, 35-52. Ed. George MacRae. Cambridge, Mass.: SBL, 1974.

Cook, Albert Stanburrough. *Biblical Quotations in Old English Prose Writers.* 2 parts. London: Macmillan, and New York: Scribner's 1898, 1903.

Crawford, S. J. "Grendel's Descent from Cain." *Modern Language*

Review, 23 (1928), 207-208.

Crook, Margaret B. *The Cruel God: Job's Search for the Meaning of Suffering.* Boston: Beacon Press, 1959.

Damon, S. Foster. *Blake's 'Job': William Blake's Illustrations of the Book of Job.* Providence: Brown University Press, 1966 (rpt. New York: E. P. Dutton, 1969).

Datz, Günther. *Die Gestalt Hiobs in der kirchlichen Exegese und der 'Arme Heinrich' Hartmanns von Aue.* Diss. Munich, n.d. Göppinger Arbeiten zur Germanistik, 108. Göppingen: Alfred Kümmerle, 1973.

Denis, Valentin. "Saint Job patron de musiciens." *Revue belge d'archéologie et d'histoire d'art*, 21 (1952), 253-298.

Dhorme, Paul. "Ecclésiaste ou Job?" *Revue biblique*, 32 (1923), 5-27.

———. *Le Livre de Job.* Paris: Victor Lecoffre, 1926. Trans. Harold Knight. London: Nelson, 1967.

Dieu, L. "Nouveaux fragments préhexaplaires du livre de Job en copte sahidique." *Le Muséon*, 13 (1912), 147-185.

Dillon, Bert. *A Chaucer Dictionary: Proper Names and Allusions, Excluding Place Names.* Boston: G. K. Hall, 1974.

Dillon, Emile Joseph. *The Original Poem of Job, Translated from the Restored Text.* London: T. Fisher Unwin, 1905.

Driver, Samuel Rolles, and George Buchanan Gray. *A Critical and Exegetical Commentary on the Book of Job.* 2 parts. The International Critical Commentary. Edinburgh: T. & T. Clark, 1921.

Dubois, Marguerite-Marie. *Les Éléments Latins dans la poésie religieuse de Cynewulf.* Paris: E. Droz, 1943.

Dudden, F. Holmes. *Gregory the Great: His Place in History and Thought.* 2 vols. London: Longmans, Green, & Co., 1905.

Eissfeldt, Otto. *The Old Testament, Including the Apocrypha and Pseudepigrapha, and Also the Works of Similar Type from Qumran: The History of the Formation of the Old Testament.* Trans. from the 3rd German edition by Peter R. Ackroyd. Oxford: Basil Blackwell, 1966.

Encyclopaedia Judaica. Ed. Cecil Roth. 16 vols. Jerusalem: Macmillan, 1972.

Faur, José. "Reflections on Job and Situation Mortality." *Judaism*, 19 (1970), 219-225.

Feinberg, Charles L. "The Poetic Structure of the Book of Job and the Ugaritic Literature." *Bibliotheca Sacra*, 103 (1946), 283-292.

Fine, Hillel A. "The Tradition of a Patient Job." *JBL*, 74 (1955), 28-32.

Fohrer, G. "Zur Vorgeschichte und Komposition des Buches Hiob." *VT*, 6 (1956), 249-267.

———. "Nun aber hat mein Auge dich geschaut: Der innere Aufbau des Buches Hiob." *Theologische Zeitschrift*, 15 (1959), 1-21.

Foster, F. H. "Is the Book of Job a Translation from an Arabic Original?" *AJSLL*, 49 (1932), 21-45.

Frankfort, Henri. *Ancient Egyptian Religion: An Interpretation.* New York: Columbia University Press, 1948 (rpt. New York: Harper Torchbooks, 1961).

Freedman, D. N. "The Elihu Speeches in the Book of Job: A Hypothetical Episode in the Literary History of the Work." *Harvard Theological Review*, 61 (1968), 51-59.

Frye, Northrop. *Anatomy of Criticism: Four Essays.* Princeton: Princeton University Press, 1957 (rpt. New York: Atheneum, 1969).

Fullerton, Kember. "The Original Conclusion of the Book of Job." *ZAW*, 1 (1924), 116-136.

Gard, Donald H. *The Exegetical Method of the Greek Translator of the Book of Job.* JBL Monograph Series, 8. Philadelphia: SBL, 1952.

———. "The Concept of Job's Character According to the Greek Translator of the Hebrew Text." *JBL*, 72 (1953), 182-186.

Gehman, Henry S. "The Theological Approach of the Greek Translator of Job 1-15." *JBL*, 68 (1949), 231-240.

Genung, John F. *The Epic of the Inner Life: Being the Book of Job.* Boston: Houghton Mifflin Co., 1891.

Gerleman, Gillis. *Studies in the Septuagint, I: The Book of Job.* Lunds Universitets Årsskrift, n.s. 1, vol. 43, part 2. Lund: Gleerup, 1947.

Gerould, Gordon Hall. "Forerunners, Congeners, and Derivatives of the Eustace Legend." *Publications of the MLA*, 19 (1904), 335-448.

Ginzberg, Louis. *The Legends of the Jews.* 7 vols. Philadelphia: Jewish Publication Society, 1909-1938.

Gioia, Louis L. "Bibliography of Editions and Translations in Progress." *Speculum*, 50 (1975), 171-188.

Glatzer, Nahum N. " 'Knowest Thou?' Notes on the Book of Job." In *Studies in Rationalism, Judaism, and Universalism, in Memory of Leon Roth*, pp. 73-86. Ed. Raphael Loewe. London: Routledge & Kegan Paul, 1966.

———. "The Book of Job and Its Interpreters." In *Biblical Motifs: Origins and Transformations*, pp. 197-220. Ed. Alexander Altman. Brandeis University Studies and Texts, 3. Cambridge: Philip W. Lown Institute of Advanced Judaic Studies, 1966.

———. *The Dimensions of Job: A Study and Selected Readings.* New York: Schocken Books, 1969.

Goitein, Lionel. "The Importance of the Book of Job for Analytic Thought." *American Imago*, 11 (1954), 407-415.

Goldsmith, Margaret E. *The Mode and Meaning of 'Beowulf.'* London: Athlone Press, 1970.

Good, Edwin M. "Job and the Literary Task: A Response." *Soundings: An Interdisciplinary Journal*, 56 (1973), 470-484.

Goodheart, Eugene. "Job and Romanticism." *The Reconstructionist*, 24 (1958-1959), 7-12.

Gooding, D. W. "Aristeas and Septuagint Origins: A Review of Recent Studies." *VT*, 13 (1963), 357-379.

Gordis, Robert. *The Book of God and Man: A Study of Job.* Chicago and London: University of Chicago Press, 1965.

Gossman, Ann. "Samson, Job, and 'the Exercise of Saints.' " *English Studies*, 45 (1964), 212-224.

Grubl, Emily Doris. *Studien zu den angelsächsischen Elegien.* Marburg: Elwert-Gräfe u. Unzer, 1948.

Guillaume, Alfred. "The Unity of the Book of Job." In *The Annual of Leeds University Oriental Society*, IV (1962-1963), pp. 26-46. Leiden: E. J. Brill, 1964.

———. *Studies in the Book of Job.* Leiden: E. J. Brill, 1968.

Hanson, Anthony, and Miriam Hanson. *The Book of Job: Introduction and Commentary.* London: SCM, 1953.

Harbage, Alfred. *Annals of English Drama: 975-1700.* Rev. edition by Samuel Schoenbaum. London: Methuen & Co., 1964.

Hartt, Frederick. " Carpaccio's Meditation on the Passion." *AB*, 22 (1940), 25-35.

Hatch, Edwin. "On Origen's Revision of the LXX text of Job." In *Essays in Biblical Greek*, pp. 215-245. Oxford: Clarendon Press, 1889.

Hausen, Adelheid. *Hiob in der französischen Literatur: Zur Rezeption eines alttestamentlichen Buches.* Europäische Hochschulschriften, Reihe XIII, 17. Bern: Herbert Lang, and Frankfurt a. M.: Peter Lang, 1972.

Hebaisha, H. A. K. "Biblical Poems from 1538-1638, with Special Reference to Poems on David and on Job." Diss. University of London (Birkbeck College), 1966.

Heffernan, Thomas J. "An Analysis of the Narrative Motifs in the

Legend of St. Eustace." *Medievalia et humanistica*, n.s. 6 (1975), 63-89.

Hone, Ralph E. *The Voice out of the Whirlwind: The Book of Job: Materials for Analysis.* San Francisco: Chandler, 1960.

Humbert, Paul. "Le modernisme de Job." *SVT*, 3 (1955), 150-161.

Hurvitz, Avi. "The Date of the Prose-Tale of Job Linguistically Reconsidered." *Harvard Theological Review*, 67 (1974), 17-34.

Irwin, William A. "An Examination of the Progress of Thought in the Dialogue of Job." *Journal of Religion*, 13 (1933), 150-164.

———. "Poetic Structure in the Dialogue of Job." *Journal of Near Eastern Studies*, 5 (1946), 26-39.

———. "Job and Prometheus." *Journal of Religion*, 30 (1950), 90-108.

———. "Job's Redeemer." *JBL*, 81 (1962), 217-229.

Jellicoe, Sidney. *The Septuagint and Modern Study.* Oxford: Clarendon Press, 1968.

The Jewish Encyclopedia. Ed. Isidore Singer. 12 vols. New York and London: Funk and Wagnalls, 1901-1912.

Kallen, Horace Meyer. *The Book of Job as a Greek Tragedy.* New York: Moffat, Yard, & Co., 1918 (rpt. New York: Hill and Wang, 1959).

Karsten, Torsten Evert. *Die mitteldeutsche poetische Paraphrase des Buches Hiob.* Berlin: Weidmann, 1910.

Kaske, R. E. "*Beowulf* and the Book of Enoch." *Speculum*, 46 (1971), 421-431.

Katzenellenbogen, Adolf. *Allegories of the Virtues and Vices in Mediaeval Art, from Early Christian Times to the Thirteenth Century.* London: The Warburg Institute, 1939.

Kaufmann, Herman Ezechiel. *Die Anwendung des Buches Hiob in der Rabbinischen Agadah.* Part 1. Frankfurt a. M., 1893.

Kautzsch, Karl. *Das sogenannte Volksbuch von Job und der Ursprung von Hiob Cap. I. II. XLII, 7-17: Ein Beitrag zur Frage Nach der Integrität des Buches Hiob.* Tübingen: J. C. B. Mohr, 1900.

Kee, Howard C. "Satan, Magic, and Salvation in the Testament of Job." *SBL Seminar Papers*, I, 53-76. Ed. George MacRae. Cambridge: SBL, 1974.

Ker, Neil Ripley. *Catalogue of Manuscripts Containing Anglo-Saxon.* Oxford: Clarendon Press, 1957.

Kierkegaard, Søren. *Repetition: An Essay in Experimental Psychology.* Trans. Walter Lowrie. Princeton: Princeton University

Press, 1941 (rpt. New York: Harper Torchbooks, 1964).

Knox, Bernard. "Sophocles' Oedipus." In *Tragic Themes in Western Literature*, pp. 7-29. Ed. Cleanth Brooks. New Haven: Yale University Press, 1955.

Kuhl, Kurt. "Neuere Literaturkritik des Buches Hiob." *Theologische Rundschau*, 21 (1953), 163-205, 257-317.

Kurtz, Benjamin P. "Gifer the Worm: An Essay toward the History of an Idea." *University of California Publications in English*, 2 (1929), 235-261.

Laistner, Max L. W. *Thought and Letters in Western Europe: A.D. 500 to 900.* London: Methuen, 1931 (rpt. Ithaca, N.Y.: Cornell University Press, 1966).

Laks, H. Joel. "The Enigma of Job: Maimonides and the Moderns." *JBL*, 83 (1964), 345-364.

Landrum, Grace Warren. "Chaucer's Use of the Vulgate." Diss. Radcliffe College, 1921.

Landsberger, Julius. *Das Buch Hiob und Goethes Faust.* Darmstadt: Ionghaus, 1882.

Lannois, Maurice "Job sa femme et les musiciens." *Aesculape*, 29 (1939), 194-207.

Lannois, Maurice, and J. Lacassagne. "Quelques représentations sculpturales du Saint homme Job." *Aesculape*, 28 (1938), 32-46.

Larcher, C. *Le Livre de Job.* 2nd rev. ed. La Sainte Bible traduite en français sous la direction de l'École Biblique de Jérusalem. Paris: Les Editions du Cerf, 1957.

Leclercq, Henri. "Job." In *Dictionnaire d'archéologie chrétienne et de liturgie.* Ed. Fernand Cabrol et al. 15 vols. Paris: Letouzey et Ané, 1903-1953.

Levenson, Jon Douglas. *The Book of Job in Its Time and in the Twentieth Century.* The LeBaron Russell Briggs Prize Honors Essay in English, 1971. Cambridge: Harvard University Press, 1972.

Lewalski, Barbara Kiefer. *Milton's Brief Epic: The Genre, Meaning, and Art of Paradise Regained.* Providence: Brown University Press, and London: Methuen, 1966.

Lindblom, Johannes. "Job and Prometheus: A Comparative Study" In *Dragma: Skrifter Utgivna av Svenska Institutet I Rom Acta Insitute Romani Regni Sueciae*, pp. 280-287. Series altera, 1. (Nilsson Festscrift), 1939.

Lods, Adolphe. "Recherches récentes [1920-34] sur le livre de Job." *Revue d'histoire et de philosophie religieuses*, 14 (1934), 501-533.

Lowth, Robert. *Lectures on the Sacred Poetry of the Hebrews.*

Trans. and ed. George Gregory. 2nd ed. Boston, 1815. (Lecture 32, "Of the Poem of Job," rpt. in Hone, pp. 175-192.)

MacDonald, Duncan Black. "Some External Evidence on the Original Form of the Legend of Job." *AJSLL*, 14 (1897-1898), 137-164.

———. "The Book of Job as Lyric." In *The Hebrew Literary Genius: An Interpretation Being an Introduction to the Reading of the Old Testament*, pp. 20-32. Princeton: Princeton University Press, 1933.

Mandelkern, Solomon. *Veteris Testamenti Concordantiae Hebraicae atque Chaldaicae*. Jerusalem and Tel Aviv: Schocken, 1969.

Mandl, Armin. *Die Peschittha zu Hiob: Nebst einem Anhang über ihr Verhältniss zu LXX und Targum*. Diss. Leipzig, 1892. Budapest: Leo Propper, 1892.

Mansi, Giovanni Domenico. *Sacrorum Conciliorum Nova et Amplissima Collectio*. 55 vols. Florence, Venice, and Paris, 1759-1962.

Martin-Achard, Robert. *From Death to Life: A Study of the Doctrine of the Resurrection in the Old Testament*, pp. 166-180. Trans. John Penney Smith. Edinburgh: Oliver & Boyd, 1960.

Meek, T. J. "Job 19.25-27." *VT* 6 (1956), 100-103.

Meiss, Millard. *Painting in Florence and Siena After the Black Death: The Arts, Religion, and Society in the Mid-Fourteenth Century*. Princeton: Princeton University Press, 1951 (rpt. New York: Harper Torchbooks, 1964).

Mendes de Castro, J. "Versão medieval inedita do Livro de Job." *Didaskalia: Revista da Faculdade de Teologia de Lisboa*, 3 (1973), 83-131.

Meyer, Kathi. "St. Job as a Patron of Music." *AB*, 36 (1954), 21-31.

Morrell, Minnie Cate. *A Manual of Old English Biblical Materials*. Knoxville: University of Tennessee Press, 1965.

Murdoch, Brian. "Genesis and Pseudo-Genesis in Late Medieval German Poetry." *Medium Ævum*, 45 (1976), 70-78.

Murray, Gilbert. *Aeschylus: The Creator of Tragedy*, pp. 87-110. Oxford: Clarendon Press, 1940.

Neuss, Paula. "Active and Idle Language: Dramatic Images in 'Mankind.' " In *Medieval Drama*, pp. 67. Ed. Neville Denny. Stratford-upon-Avon Studies, 16. London: Edward Arnold, 1973.

Noth, Martin. "Noah, Daniel und Hiob in Ezechiel xiv." *VT*, 1 (1951), 251-260.

Noth, Martin, and D. Winton Thomas, eds. *Wisdom in Israel and in the Ancient Near East: Presented to Professor Harold Henry Rowley . . . in Celebration of his Sixtyfifth Birthday. SVT*, 3. Leiden: E. J. Brill, 1955.

Oesterley, William O. E., and Theodore Henry Robinson. *An Introduction to the Books of the Old Testament*, pp. 166-178. London: SPCK, 1934.

Ogilvy, Jack D. A. *Books Known to the English, 597-1066*. Mediaeval Academy of America Publications, 76. Cambridge, Mass.: Mediaeval Academy of America, 1967.

Orlinsky, Harry M. "Studies in the Septuagint of the Book of Job." *HUCA*, 28 (1957), 53-74; 29 (1958), 229-271; 30 (1959), 153-167; 32 (1961), 239-268; 33 (1962), 119-151.

von der Osten, Gert. "Job and Christ: The Development of a devotional Image." *JWCI*, 16 (1953), 153-158.

Otto, Rudolph. *The Idea of the Holy: An Inquiry into the Non-Rational Factor in the Idea of the Divine and Its Relation to the Rational*. Trans. John W. Harvey. Rev. ed. London: Oxford University Press, 1928.

Paulus, Jean. "Le thème du juste souffrant dans la pensée grecque et hébraïque." *Revue de l'histoire des religions*, 121 (1940), 18-66.

Peake, Arthur S. *The Problem of Suffering in the Old Testament*. The Hartley Lecture Delivered to the Primitive Methodist Conference in Carr's Lane Chapel, Birmingham, June 8, 1904. London: Robert Bryant, 1904.

Perrow, Eber Carle. "The Last Will and Testament as a Form of Literature." *Transactions of the Wisconsin Academy of Sciences, Arts and Letters*, 17 (1913), part I, 682-753.

Pfeiffer, Robert. "Edomitic Wisdom." *ZAW*, n. s. 3 (1926), 13-25.

———. *Introduction to the Old Testament*, pp. 660-707. Rev. ed. London: Adam and Charles Black, 1948.

Philonenko, Marc. "Le *Testament de Job* et les Thérapeutes." *Semitica: Cahiers publiés par l'Institut d'études sémitiques de l'Université de Paris*, 8 (1958), 41-53.

Pinto, Lucille. "The Worm Charm in the Middle Ages." Diss. University of Chicago, 1969.

Poesch, Jessie. "The Beasts from Job in the *Liber Floridus* Manuscripts." *JWCI*, 33 (1970), 41-51.

Prado, J. "La perspectiva escatólogica en Job 19, 25-27." *Estudios Bíblicos*, 25 (1966), 5-39.

von Rad, Gerhard. "Hiob xxviii und die altägyptische Weisheit." *SVT*, 3 (1955), 293-301.

Rand, Edward Kennard. *Founders of the Middle Ages.* Cambridge: Harvard University Press, 1928.

Rankin, Oliver Shaw. *Israel's Wisdom Literature: Its Bearing on Theology and the History of Religion.* Kerr Lectures delivered in Trinity College, Glasgow, 1933-1936. Edinburgh: T & T Clark, 1936 (rpt. New York: Schocken, 1969).

Réau, Louis. *Iconographie de l'art chrétien.* 3 vols. in 6 parts. Paris: Presses universitaires, 1956.

Reid, Stephen A. "The Book of Job." *Psychoanalytic Review*, 60 (1973-1974), 373-391.

Richter, Heinz. "Die Naturweisheit des Alten Testaments im Buche Hiob." *ZAW*, 70 (1958), 1-20.

Robertson, David. "The Book of Job: A Literary Study." *Soundings: An Interdisciplinary Journal*, 56 (1973), 446-469.

Robinson, H. Wheeler. *The Religious Ideas of the Old Testament.* London: Duckworth, 1913.

Rollet, J. "La Maladie de Job." *Aesculape*, 15 (1925), 90-95.

Rowley, Harold Henry. "The Book of Job and Its Meaning." *Bulletin of the John Rylands Library*, 41 (1958), 167-207.

Russell, D. S. *The Method and Message of Jewish Apocalyptic: 200 B.C.-A.D. 100.* Philadelphia: Westminster, 1964.

Sanders, Paul S., ed. *Twentieth Century Interpretations of the Book of Job: A Collection of Critical Essays.* Englewood Cliffs, N. J.: Prentice-Hall, 1968.

Sarna, Nahum M. "Epic Substratum in the Prose of Job." *JBL*, 76 (1957), 13-25.

Scholem, Gershom. *Sabbatai Ṣevi: The Mystical Messiah.* Trans. R. J. Zwi Werblowsky. Bollingen Series, 93. Princeton: Princeton University Press, 1973 (rpt. 1975).

Severs, J. Burke. "The Job Passage in the *Clerkes Tale.*" *Modern Language Notes*, 49 (1934), 461-462.

———, ed. *A Manual of the Writings in Middle English: 1050-1500*, I, part 1: "Romances." New Haven: The Connecticut Academy of Arts and Sciences, 1967.

———. *A Manual of the Writings in Middle English: 1050-1500*, II, part 2: "The *Pearl* Poet"; part 3: "Wyclyf and His followers"; part 4: "Translations and Paraphrases of the Bible and Commentaries"; part 5: "Saints' Legends"; part 6: "Instructions for Religious." Hamden: The Shoe String Press (for the Connecticut Academy of Arts and Sciences), 1970.

Sewall, Richard B. *The Vision of Tragedy*, pp. 9-24. New Haven: Yale University Press, 1959.

Shepherd, Geoffrey. "Scriptural Poetry." In *Continuations and Beginnings: Studies in Old English Literature*, pp. 1-36. Ed. Eric Gerald Stanely. London: Nelson, 1966.

Shires, Henry M. *Finding the Old Testament in the New*. Philadelphia: Westminster, 1974.

Siger, Leonard. "The Image of Job in the Renaissance." Diss. Johns Hopkins University, 1960.

Silverstein, Theodore, ed. *Visio Sancti Pauli: The History of the Apocalypse in Latin, Together with Nine Texts*. Studies and Documents, 4. London: Christophers, 1935.

———. "The Vision of St. Paul: New Links and Patterns in the Western Tradition." *Archives d'histoire doctrinale et littéraire du moyen âge*, 34 (1959), 199-248.

Smalley, Beryl. *The Study of the Bible in the Middle Ages*. 2nd ed. Oxford: Blackwell, 1952.

Smith, Macklin. *Prudentius'* Psychomachia: *A Reexamination*. Princeton: Princeton University Press, 1976.

Smyth, Mary W. *Biblical Quotations in Middle English Literature before 1300*. Yale Studies in English, 41. New York: Henry Holt, 1911.

Sokoloff, Michael. *The Targum to Job from Qumran Cave XI*. Bar-Ilan Studies in Near Eastern Languages and Culture. Jerusalem: Ahva Press, 1974.

Speer, Julius. "Zur Exegese von Hiob 19, 25-27." *ZAW*, 25 (1905), 47-140.

Spicq, Ceslaus. *Esquisse d'une histoire de l'exégèse latine au moyen âge*. Bibliothèque Thomiste, 26. Paris: J. Vrin, 1944.

Spiegel, Shalom. "Noah, Daniel, and Job, Touching on Canaanite Relics in the Legends of the Jews." In *Louis Ginzberg Jubilee Volume: On the Occasion of His Seventieth Birthday*, pp. 305-355. New York: American Academy for Jewish Research, 1945.

Stanford, William Bedell. *The Ulysses Theme: A Study in the Adaptability of a Traditional Hero*. 2nd ed. Oxford: Blackwell & Mott, 1963 (rpt. Ann Arbor: University of Michigan Press, 1968).

Staples, William Ewart. *The Speeches of Elihu: A Study of Job xxxii-xxxvii*. University of Toronto Studies, Philological Series, 8. Toronto: University of Toronto Press, 1924.

Steadman, John M. "Leviathan and Renaissance Etymology." *Journal of the History of Ideas*, 28 (1967), 575-576.

Stein, Robert A. "The Sources and Implications of the Jobean Analogies in *Paradise Regained.*" *Anglia,* 88 (1970), 323-333.

Stettiner, Richard. *Die illustrierten Prudentiushandschriften.* 2 vols. Berlin: Preuss, 1895 (text); Berlin: Grote, 1905 (plates).

Stevenson, William Barron. *The Poem of Job: A Literary Study with a New Translation.* The Schweich Lectures of the British Academy, 1943. London: Oxford University Press, 1947.

———. *Critical Notes on the Hebrew Text of the Poem of Job.* Aberdeen: Aberdeen University Press, 1951.

Stockhammer, Morris. "The Righteousness of Job." *Judaism,* 7 (1958), 64-71.

Studer, G. L. "Über die Integrität des Buches Hiob." *Jahrbücher für protestantische Theologie,* 1 (1875), 688-723.

"Studies in the Book of Job." *Semeia: An Experimental Journal for Biblical Criticism,* 7 (1977). Ed. Robert Polzin and David Robertson.

Swete, Henry Barclay. *An Introduction to the Old Testament in Greek, with an Appendix Containing the Letter of Aristeas.* Ed. H. St. J. Thackeray. 2nd ed. rev. by Richard Rusden Ottley. Cambridge: Cambridge University Press, 1914.

Talmon, Shemaryahu. " 'Wisdom' in the Book of Esther." *VT,* 13 (1963), 419-455.

Teunissen, John James. "Of Patience and Heroic Martyrdom: The Book of Job and Milton's Conception of Patient Suffering in *Paradise Regained* and *Samson Agonistes.*" Diss. The University of Rochester, 1967.

Tsevat, Matitiahu. "The Meaning of the Book of Job." *HUCA,* 37 (1966), 73-106.

Tur-Sinai, Naphtali Herz (H. Torczyner). *The Book of Job: A New Commentary.* Rev. ed. Jerusalem: Kiryath Sepher, 1967.

Usmiani, Renate. "A New Look at the Drama of 'Job.' " *Modern Drama,* 13 (1970-1971), 191-200.

Vaccari, Alberto. "Scripsitne Beda commentarium in Job?" *Biblica: Commentarii editi a Pontificio Instituto Biblico,* 5 (1924), 369-373.

Walls, Alfred. *The Oldest Drama in the World: The Book of Job Arranged in Dramatic Form with Elucidations.* New York: Hunt & Eaton, 1891.

Wang, Andreas. *Der "Miles Christianus" im 16. und 17. Jahrhundert und seine mittelalterliche Tradition: Ein Beitrag zum Ver-*

hältnis von sprachlicher und graphischer Bildlichkeit. Mikrokosmos: Beiträge zur Literaturwissenschaft und Bedeutungsforschung, 1. Bern and Frankfurt a. M.: Herbert and Peter Lang, 1975.

Wasselynck, René. "Les compilations des 'Moralia in Job' du VIIe au XIIe siècle." *RTAM*, 29 (1962), 5-32.

———. "Les 'Moralia in Job' dans les ouvrages de morale du haut moyen âge latin." *RTAM*, 31 (1964), 5-31.

———. "L'influence de l'exégèse de S. Grégoire le Grand sur les commentaires bibliques médiévaux (VIIe - XIIe s.)." *RTAM*, 32 (1965), 157-204.

———. "La présence des Moralia de S. Grégoire le Grand dans les ouvrages de morale du XIIe siècle." *RTAM*, 35 (1968), 197-240; 36 (1969), 31-45.

Waterman, Leroy. "Note on Job 19, 23-27: Job's Triumph of Faith." *JBL*, 69 (1950), 379-380.

Weisbach, Werner. "L'Histoire de Job dans les Arts." *Gazette des beaux-arts*, 16 (1936), 102-112.

Wertheimer, Shlomoh Aharon, ed. *Batei Midrashot: Twenty-Five Midrashim Published for the First Time from MSS Discovered in the Genizoth of Jerusalem and Egypt*, II, 157-186. 2nd ed. Abraham Wertheimer. Jerusalem: Mosad Harav Kook, 1953.

Wetzstein, J. G. "The Monastery of Job in Hauran, and the Tradition of Job." In Franz J. Delitzsch, *Biblical Commentary on the Book of Job*, II, 395-450. Trans. Francis Bolton. 2 vols. 2nd ed. rev. Clark's Foreign Theological Library, 4th ser., 10, 11. Edinburgh: T & T Clark, 1866, 1869.

Wielandt, Ulf. *Hiob in der alt- und mittelhochdeutschen Literatur.* Diss. Albert-Ludwigs-Universität zu Freiburg i. Br., 1970. Bamberg: Rodenbusch, n.d.

Wiernikowski, Isaak. *Das Buch Hiob nach der Auffassung der rabbinischen Literatur in den ersten fünf nachchristlichen Jahrhunderten*, part 1. Breslau: H. Fleischmann, 1902.

Wirszubski, Chaim. "Giovanni Pico's Book of Job." *JWCI*, 32 (1969), 171-199.

Withycombe, Elizabeth Gidley. *The Oxford Dictionary of English Christian Names.* 2nd ed. Oxford: Clarendon Press, 1950 (rpt. 1963).

van der Woude, A. S. "Das Hiobtargum aus Qumran Höhle XI." *SVT*, 9 (1962), 322-331.

Wright, Andrew. *Blake's 'Job': A Commentary.* Oxford: Clarendon Press, 1972.

Wright, Nathalia. *Melville's Use of the Bible, with a New Appendix by the Author.* New York: Octagon, 1969.

Zhitlowsky, Chaim. *Job and Faust.* Trans. and ed. Percy Matenko. In *Two Studies in Yiddish Culture,* pp. 71-162. Ed Percy Matenko and Samuel Sloan. Leiden: E. J. Brill, 1968.

Zink, James E. "Impatient Job: An Interpretation of Job 19, 25-27." *JBL,* 84 (1965), 147-152.

Notes

Introduction

1. In the introduction and chapter 1, translations of the Hebrew Book of Job and other biblical texts are, unless otherwise indicated, taken from the New English Bible. Hebrew words and phrases are cited from the Masoretic version. Citations of the Septuagint Book of Job are from the Thomson translation, ed. C. A. Muses. Biblical quotations in chapter 2 and following are, unless otherwise indicated, taken from the Vulgate and glossed by the English Douay translation.

2. For a survey of references to Job in medieval Latin, Middle English, Old French, and Middle High German, see M. Allen, pp. 52-74, 339-346 (I am indebted to Professor George Kane of the University of North Carolina for drawing my attention to this dissertation written under his supervision); Besserman (1973[1]), pp. 65-213; Datz, pp. 95-177; Hausen, pp. 39-260; and Wielandt, pp. 34-143. The article on the Book of Job in the *Encyclopaedia Judaica,* besides providing an excellent introduction to textual and literary problems in the biblical story, includes a brief discussion of the later history of the Job legend in literature and art.

3. Aspects of the legacy of the Job legend in Western art have been discussed by Bandmann, Budde, Denis, Hartt, Meyer, von der Osten, Poesch, Réau, and Weisbach.

1. Biblical Origins

1. On the place of Job in the Jewish canon, see Gordis, pp. 220-222; and on Job in the Christian canon, see Dhorme (1926), pp. vii-xii and Swete, p. 228.

2. The discussion of wisdom literature which follows is based primarily on Noth and Thomas, Rankin, Richter, and Talmon.

3. For a list of passages in Ecclesiastes and other wisdom books which resemble passages in Job, see Driver and Gray, p. lxviii; and on thematic affinities between Ecclesiastes and Job, see Dhorme (1923). The Egyptian influence on Ecclesiastes is now considered by many to be paramount (see

Eissfeldt, pp. 498-499); on the question of Egyptian, Greek, or other influences on Job, see *Job*, ed. Pope, pp. lvi-lxxi.

4. On the verse structure of the Book of Job, see Irwin (1946); and *Job*, ed. Pope, pp. l-lvi.

5. This is the view of Alt, Fohrer (1956), and Sarna, among others. A survey of the relevant scholarship appears in Rowley, pp. 177-186. Most recently Hurvitz has argued that certain words and expressions in the prose parts of Job are not classical Hebrew but late-biblical.

6. A number of studies try to establish a historical context for the poem as an expression of Israelite history and nationalist concerns (see *Job*, ed. Pope, p. xxxv, nn. 32 and 32a). Guillaume (1968), esp. pp. 7-14, argues ingeniously for a mid-sixth-century date and for a very precisely drawn setting of the poem: a Hebrew-Arab enclave in the Hijaz that is suffering at the hands of Babylonian invaders in the time of Babylon's last king, Nabonidus.

For various rabbinical attempts to place Job in the patriarchal period, in the time of Moses, the Judges, or even in the Persian period, and for debate about whether or not he was an Israelite, see *BT*, Baba Batra, 14b-16b.

7. As quoted in *Job*, ed. Pope, p. 354, with the comment that "these traditions are garbled and of dubious value."

8. For the classic discussion of this "fraught-with-background" quality of biblical narratives—specifically Genesis but applicable also to Job—see Auerbach, pp. 1-20 (esp. pp. 9-10); and on the attempt to fill in Job's background in the *Testament of Job*, see chapter 2, below. On Aramaic and Coptic versions of the Job legend, see Bacher; Dhorme (1926), pp. cxcvi-ccxx; Dieu; Mandl; *Livre de Job*, trans. and ed. Porcher; Sokoloff; and van der Woude. On Job in Arabic literature, see the Koran, Suras 4:161, 6:84, 21:83-84, and 38:40-45; Apt; MacDonald (1897-1898); and *Testament of Job*, ed. Kohler, pp. 292-295.

The Jewish legendary material on Job is conveniently assembled in Ginzberg, II, 223-242 and V, 381-390 (notes and additional references). Also valuable is Wertheimer's reconstruction of a hypothetical "Midrash Iyyov," based on quotations in other midrashim. See also *Testament of Job*, ed. Kohler, pp. 267-270; and for the view of Job in the Talmud, see BT, Pesaḥim, 112a, Megillah, 28a, Sotah, 11a, 27b, 31a, and Baba Batra, 14b-16b. On rabbinical attitudes to Job, see Kaufmann and Wiernikowski; and for an especially good account of the ambivalence of later rabbinic writers, see Glatzer (1966[2]). For an early-twentieth-century Judeo-Arabic poem on the legend of Job reflecting much older Arabic and Jewish folk tradition, see *Histoire de notre seigneur Job*.

A notable departure from attempts in Jewish tradition to historicize the story of Job is the following comment in the Talmud: "Job never was and never existed, but is only a typical figure" (*BT*, Baba Batra, 15b). This view was echoed by the influential twelfth-century Jewish philosopher Maimonides, who denied the historicity of the Book of Job, holding instead that "its basis is a fiction, conceived for the purpose of explaining the different opinions which people hold on Divine Providence" (*Guide for the Perplexed*, p. 296).

9. Most commentators reply that this is the result of imperfect melding of originally independent prose and poetic texts (see n. 5, above).

10. Zophar begins with an angry rebuke of Job, as does Bildad. Only Eliphaz is mild, at least initially. He is the only one of the comforters whom the Lord addresses by name, as if he were their spokesman or representative (42:7). For analysis of ostensible differences in tone and content of the comforters' speeches, see Irwin (1933) and Crook, pp. 27-117. It seems to me, however, that the substantial identity of the comforters' views is in the end more significant than their minor differences.

11. For a sampling of the majority opinion that the Elihu speeches are the work of a later author, see *Job*, ed. Pope, pp. xxvii-xxviii, 241, nn. 1-2, 247, n. 1; and Staples. And for the view that the Elihu speeches are original and, indeed, thematically central, see Gordis, pp. 104-116; Guillaume (1964), pp. 31-35; and Freedman, who argues ingeniously for an original distribution of Elihu's speeches at strategic points in the dialogue.

12. Some of the many suggestions for rearranging the dialogue to form three complete cycles are reviewed by Lods, pp. 504-508; Pfeiffer (1948), p. 671; and Rowley, p. 188, nn. 1-2. Stevenson's suggested rearrangement (1951, pp. 123 ff) is representative of the more reasonable efforts along these lines. Baumgärtel (pp. 157-165), who would limit the original dialogue to just a few verses, represents a more radical school of thought.

13. *Job*, ed. Pope, p. xxvii, leans toward the generally accepted view that the wisdom poem is extraneous, but admits its stylistic and thematic affinities with the dialogues. Fine, however, considers it another manifestation of Job's patience, along with the prologue and chapter 27. Baeck (pp. 95-100) sees it as a key to the poem's meaning. For an account of its Near Eastern literary milieu, see von Rad.

14. The question of its genre has engendered some of the most exciting discussion about the Book of Job. Among the studies treating the poem as drama, Horace Kallen's *The Book of Job as a Greek Tragedy* has achieved deserved renown, even if its arguments are no longer as persuasive as they once may have been. Other studies include: Bradley, who indentifies features of epic, drama, and parable in the poem; Buttenweiser, who sees it as a drama; Feinberg, who links Job with Ugaritic epic literature; Genung, who also sees it primarily as epic; MacDonald (1933), who concentrates on the lyric element; Sewall, who makes some interesting observations about the tragic elements in the poem; and Walls, who sees it as a drama. Also common are studies linking Job with Prometheus or other classical heroes, though these usually treat characterization rather than genre (for example, Bussler; Irwin, 1950; Knox; Lindblom; Murray; and Paulus). For recent essays on comedy, irony, and drama in the Book of Job, see the special volume of *Semeia* entitled "Studies in the Book of Job."

15. See Driver and Gray, pp. lxv-lxxi, for evidence placing the composition of Job in the fifth century B.C.; Pope, however, asserts that the date of the book is "still an open question" (*Job, p. xl*), and tentatively places the dialogue in the seventh century B.C. For other views, see n. 6, above.

As Jerome's remarks about the original language of the Book of Job show, the idea that Job is not pure Hebrew is not new: "Haec autem translatio nullum de veteribus sequitur interpretem, sed ex ipso hebraico arabicoque sermone et interdum syro, nunc verba, nunc sensus, nunc simul utrumque resonabit . . . Sciendum quippe Danihelem maxime et Ezram hebraicis quidem litteris, sed chaldaico sermone conscriptos, et unam Hieremiae pericopen. Iob quoque cum arabic lingua habere plurimam societatem" (*PL*, XXVIII, 1080-1081; 1291). Many scholars have posited either an Egyptian, Phoenician, Aramaic, Edomite, or Arabic original from which the Book of Job was supposedly translated (for example, Albright, 1927—but cf. Albright, 1955; Foster; Guillaume, 1968; Pfeiffer, 1926; and Tur-Sinai, pp. xxx-xl).

16. *Anatomy of Criticism*, p. 189. Though Frye speaks as a nonspecialist, there are biblical scholars who share his view. As Bič puts it: on ne peut résoudre la problématique du livre tout entier que du point de vue de sa rédaction définitive. C'est elle seulement qui nous adresse un message concret" (p. 33). Other defenders of the poem's final coherence include: Baeck, Gordis, Guillaume (1964), Faur, and Kautzsch (pp. 67-88). On the other hand, Fullerton, Pope (*Job*, pp. xxiii-xxx), and a majority of scholars deny its final coherence (see Rowley, pp. 173-192.)

17. See *Job*, ed. Pope, pp. xlv-xlvii.

18. See Glatzer (1969), p. 287; *Job*, ed. Pope, pp. lxxiii-lxxxiv; and, for a list of other scholars holding this view, Rowley, p. 195, nn. 2-3. Rowley himself, however, underplays the idea that the poem was written to deny the deuteronomic notion of God's justice (p. 200). Rankin (pp. 77-97) is even more extreme in denying a desire on the part of the author of Job to, as Robert Frost puts it in *The Masque of Reason*, "stultify the Deuteronomist."

19. For a "diagnosis" of Job's malady, see *Job*, ed. Pope, p. 21; and see further chapter 2, n. 37, below.

20. See n. 10, above; and cf. *Job*, ed. Pope, pp. lxxv-lxxx.

21. See nn. 10 and 12, above.

22. *Job*, ed. Pope, p. lxxxi. This is also Rowley's view (p. 186). It is interesting to note that the importance of Job's intercessory prayer in effecting his vindication was asserted by early rabbinic commentators (see Ginzberg, V, 389, n. 38).

23. On this point, see further E. Dillon, pp. xi-xiii, and Faur.

24. A number of scholars have recognized that Job presents several answers to the theodicy question in the course of the debates. See for example Buber, pp. 195-197; Oesterley and Robinson, pp. 166-178; and Stevenson (1947), pp. 52-55.

25. Two writers who seem to acknowledge modifications of the Deuteronomist theory in Job are Larcher, pp. 16-17; and Stockhammer, p. 65.

26. *Ancient Egyptian Religion*, p. 4. Later on in this work, Frankfort also uses the phrase "multiplicity of answers."

27. See *ANCL*, XII, p. 188.

28. This attitude toward suffering is found elsewhere in both Old and New Testaments (see Proverbs 3:11-12 and Hebrews 12:6). In later Jewish and Christian tradition, suffering came to be regarded as chastening or purgative preparation for reward in the afterlife (see Laks, pp. 354-355;

and Rankin, pp. 115-119). Christian statements of this view of suffering in relation to Job appear in the *Apostolical Constitutions*: "Receive the afflictions that fall upon thee with an even mind, and the chances of life without overmuch sorrow, knowing that a reward shall be given to thee by God, as was given to Job and to Lazarus" (*ANCL*, XVII, 182); in Ambrose, *De interpellatione Job et David, PL*, XIV, 797; Cassiodorus, *Expositio in Psalterium, PL*, LXX, 271; Gregory the Great, *Moralia*, I, 606; and in other exegetical treatises too numerous to list.

29. Commentators who take some notice of parallelism and repetition in the poem include: Peake, pp. 16-18; Sarna, pp. 18-20; and Studer, p. 698.

30. Rather than "whale," which the New English Bible proposes as a preferred alternate to Leviathan (p. 724, note b). I should also mention that ordinarily I have not adopted the transpositions of passages in the New English Bible version of the Book of Job—the traditional order of passages in the text is of primary importance for the present literary analysis. One minor exception to this practice is noted where it occurs.

31. See *Job*, ed. Pope, pp. lxxx-lxxxi.

32. Tsevat, p. 93.

33. Among the many passages in which Job and his interlocutors anticipate the Lord's words on the mysteries of nature are: 4:8-10; 9:1-10; 11:7-9; 12:7-12; 25-26:14; 28; and 36:26-37:12.

34. See for example Barton, 67; Buber, pp. 188-197; Fohrer (1959); Martin-Achard, pp. 166-180; and Otto, pp. 80-83. Kierkegaard has summed up this view of the poem's resolution in the following way: "Did Job lose his case? Yes, eternally; for he can appeal to no higher court than that which judged him. Did Job gain his case? Yes, eternally . . . for the fact that he lost his case *before God*" (*Repetition*, p. 117).

35. Pope's note on the ambiguity in the Lord's response to Job is helpful: "How could God rebuke Job for speaking in ignorance and then commend him for having spoken the truth? Some interpreters attempt to explain this difficulty by taking the word in the Hebrew to mean 'sincerity,' but the word nowhere has this sense. The basic meaning is 'correct.' The almost identical expression occurs in I Sam xxiii 23 where RSV renders 'sure information.' Delitzsch notes that objective truth and subjective truthfulness are blended in the notion of what is 'correct;' he suggests that the correct elements of Job's speeches were his denying that sin is always punished with affliction and his holding fast to his innocence despite his friends' attacks" (*Job*, p. 350).

36. From "The Book of Job," originally published in the *Westminister Review*, 1853 (rpt. in Hone, p. 222). For a more radical, twentieth-century interpretation along these lines, according to which Job is victorious not only at his comforters' but also at God's expense, see Robertson, rebutted by Good.

37. *SLNPNF*, X, 178; and cp. Gregory the Great, *Moralia*, I, 186.

38. On the textual problems in Job 19:25-27, see *Job*, ed. Pope, pp. 146-147, nn. 25a-27c.

39. For a thorough study of the exegetical tradition of Job 19:25-27, see

Speer. Other useful studies of these verses and the history of their interpretation include: Larcher, pp. 27-31; Meek; Prado; Waterman; and Zink. It is interesting to note, as Speer and others point out, that Chrysostom and his followers in the Eastern Church did not adduce these verses as Old Testament support for their views on resurrection, even though their views of the matter were in general similar to those held by the Western Fathers. And curiously enough, in Jewish tradition Job's sin was thought by some to have been his *denial* of resurrection of the dead (see *BT*, Baba Batra, 16a; and Ginzberg, II, 227).

40. *Job*, ed. Pope, p. 146, n. 25a; see also Irwin (1962).

41. *Job*, ed. Pope, p. 108, nn. 13-15, and pp. 146-147, nn. 25a-27c.

42. For an alternative translation of the second passage that lends even more support to the following argument, and for detailed discussion of the textual problems both passages present, see *Job*, ed. Pope, pp. 143-145, 227, and 238-239.

43. The theme of biblical immortality in Job is hinted at by Waterman and poetically expounded by Zhitlowsky, pp. 155-167.

44. For numerous occurrences in the Old Testament of *sefer*, "book," and related forms of the same root, some of which reflect the theme of biblical immortality (instances, that is, in which the Bible calls attention to its own authenticity and durability) see Mandelkern, pp. 804-805.

45. See the *Jewish Encyclopedia*, s.v. "Names (Personal)"; and E. G. Withycombe, s.v. "Job." In England, the use of "Job" as a Christian name came into fashion, in a limited way, after the Reformation. Bardsley, s.v. "Job," records the existence of one "Job-rakt-out-of-the-ashes," born September 1, 1611. Starting in the eighteenth century, "Job" is often used by English writers as a name for comic characters: e.g., Job Thornberry in Colman's *John Bull*, Job Vinegar in Fielding's *The Champion*, and assorted Jobs in Mrs. Gaskell's *Mary Barton*, Dickens' *Pickwick Papers* and *Our Mutual Friend*, George Eliot's *Felix Holt*, *Adam Bede*, and *Middlemarch*, and H. Rider Haggard's *She*.

46. Quoted by Glatzer (1969), p. vi; and for Kierkegaard's further thoughts along these lines, see *Repetition*, pp. 101-118.

47. Why Noah, Danel (*sic*), and Job are grouped together in these verses is elucidated by Noth (1951) and by Spiegel.

48. On allusions to Job in the Apocrypha and New Testament, consult Hanson and Hanson, pp. 22-29; Kuhl, 266-267 and nn. 1-5; and Shires, p. 219.

49. It is probable, however, that Greek transcriptions of the Hebrew Bible were in use in the third, and perhaps even the fourth, centuries B.C. On the extremely thorny question of Septuagint origins, see Swete, pp. 1-20, Gooding, and Jellicoe. And for discussion of those texts and editions of the Septuagint which have the greatest value for the study of Job, see Orlinsky, 119-125.

50. These changes have been subjected to intense scholarly scrutiny in the last few decades. Among the most important studies are those by Gard, Gehman, Gerleman, Hatch, and Orlinsky.

51. Origen, "Letter to Africanus," *ANCL*, X, 373. For the decipherment of Origen's textually problematic remark, see Orlinsky, p. 54; and on the length of the Septuagint Job, consult also Jellicoe, pp. 136-137. As Swete writes: "The evident desire of the translator to follow Classical models suggests that he was an Alexandrian Hellenist who intended his version for general reading, rather than for use in the synagogue" (p. 256).

52. Instead of Thomson's "unclean place."

53. See, for example, Stevenson (1947), p. 77; and chapter 2, n. 7, below.

54. Cited by Stevenson (1947), p. 78, trans. from Mansi, *Collectio*, IX, 223-225: "de beato Iob historiam maximam et claram, quae in ore omnium similiter ferebatur, non solum Israelitici generio sed et aliorum."

55. Mansi, *Collectio*, X, 223-225.

2. Apocryphal and Ecclesiastical Traditions

1. The Therapeutae were a Jewish monastic community living in Egypt. On the possibility of Therapeutae provenance for the *Testament*, see Philonenko (1958).

2. For an annotated chronological bibliography of *Testament* studies, see *Testament*, ed. Kraft et al., pp. 17-20. This is the edition and translation I follow in the present discussion. Still useful, though largely superceded by Kraft, are the translation and notes in Philonenko (1968), the introduction and translation in Kohler, and the introduction in the edition by James. Also valuable, though less accessible, are the introduction, translation, and notes by Spittler.

3. Instead of Kraft's "psalms."

4. On the structure of opposition and conflict in the *Testament*, see Collins.

5. For a brief account of the genre in biblical literature and a bibliography, see Eissfeldt, pp. 631-636, 775. For a survey history of the literary testament in later literature, see Perrow.

6. See Collins, p. 46. I am also indebted to Collins (pp. 37-39) for some of the ideas in the present paragraph on how the *Testament* differs from more typical testamentary compositions.

7. *Testament*, ed. James, p. xcvi.

8. See *Testament*, ed. Philonenko, pp. 10-11, for the view that in these and other details the *Testament* followed the Septuagint. For a list of scholars who believe the converse to have been the case, consult *Testament*, ed. Kraft, pp. 17-20.

9. For these as well as other analogues to motifs in the *Testament*, see *Testament*, ed. Kohler, pp. 264-295. Job's wife is also said to have been Dinah and his children given fanciful names (thought different from the ones they carry in the *Testament*) in Pseudo-Philo's *Liber antiquitatum biblicarum*, a first-century Jewish Bible history that was widely known in the Middle Ages (for the reference to Job, see Pseudo-Philo, p. 134; and on the popularity of the work, see ibid., pp. 18-22).

10. "To be an 'athlete' of godliness is often recommended in Alexandrian writings (iv. Macc. vi.10; xvii.15, 16; and in Philo, passim; cp. Hebr. x.32)," *Testament*, ed. Kohler, p. 279. See also n. 20, below.

11. On the significance of this biblical motif, see *Job*, ed. Pope, p. 353, n. 15.

12. On the importance of magic and mysticism in the *Testament*, see Kee.

13. For a more systematic account of the exegetical writings on Job, see Datz; Lewalski, pp. 10-36; and Siger, pp. 1-81. For discussion of the relationship between the recently published fourth-century commentary on Job by Julian the Arian and the Greek exegetical tradition, see Julian the Arian, *Hiobkommentar*, ed. Hagedorn.

14. See Dudden, I, 139, 243.

15. For a brief but reliable account of patristic exegetical practice and Gregory's place in the exegetical tradition, see Smalley, pp. 1-36 (esp. 32-35); and for a more detailed account of Gregory's methodology, see Dudden, II, 296-310.

16. In the former, "historical," interpretation Gregory appears to follow Ambrose. For an ingenious but ultimately unconvincing attempt to prove that Gregory's approach to the Book of Job is more "literal" than many readers tend to think, see Catry.

17. Gregory's denial of Job's righteous rebelliousness is found in *Moralia*, I, 19-21. For Ambrose's recognition of Job's problematic vehemence in protesting his fate, see *De interpellatione Job et David*, *PL*, XIV, 797. Although, by contrast with Ambrose, Gregory appears at pains to explain away Job's blasphemous or nearly blasphemous remarks, he does acknowledge that Job complained somewhat: "lest by his very insensitivity he should show a contempt of God" (*Moralia*, I, 88).

18. For a list of Gregory's frequent reiterations of Job's saintly patience and his prefigurement of Christ, see *Moralia*, III, part 2, index, s.v. "Patience" and "Christ." As the writers cited in n. 13, above, have shown, these are two themes that dominate the entire exegetical Job tradition. Some early exponents of Job's perfect patience include: Tertullian, *De patientia*, *PL*, I, 1270-1271; Cyprian, *De bono patientia*, *PL*, IV, 633-634; and Augustine, *De patientia*, *PL*, XL, 615-616. And for early promulgators of the typological equation Job=Christ, see: Jerome, *Commentarii*, *PL*, XXVI, 801-802; Zeno of Verona, *Tractatus XV*, *PL*, XI, 439-443; and see further in Datz, pp. 150-153. The identification of Job and Jesus found further support in frequent patristic contrasts of each of them to Adam (for details, see Lewalski, pp. 178-179; and Siger, pp. 11-12). On Job as a messiah figure in seventeenth-century Jewish mystical writings, see Scholem, pp. 308-310.

19. *Moralia*, III, part 2, index, s.v. "Devil," "Wife," "Friends"; and for other exegetical opinions, most of which—earlier as well as later—are in harmony with Gregory's, see Datz, pp. 108-111 and 119-124.

20. See *Moralia*, I, 20, 23, 34, 575, and further in III, part 2, index, s.v. "Athlete," "Soldier of god"; and for other exegetical pronouncements on

Job's role as wrestler/warrior/athlete/*miles christi*, see Datz, pp. 135-137; Lewalski, pp. 22-26 (where the tradition is traced from the early Christian centuries into the Protestant exegesis of the seventeenth century); and Wang, pp. 140-144.

21. *Moralia*, III, part 2, index, s.v. "Resurrection"; and further in Datz, pp. 148-150; and Siger, pp. 7-9.

22. *Moralia*, III, part 2, index, s.v. "Behemoth" and "Leviathan"; and further in Datz, pp. 126-128. On the place of Behemoth and Leviathan in Jewish tradition, where they sometimes figure as beasts to be consumed at the messianic banquet, see Russell, pp. 123-125, 294.

23. See Dudden, I, 195-196; and Laistner, pp. 107-108.

24. For discussion of the influence of the *Moralia* on the *Glossa ordinaria* and other works, see Dudden, I, 195-196, and the important series of articles by Wasselynck.

25. The shift to a more literal exegetical approach to Job, beginning in the thirteenth century and growing steadily into the seventeenth, is treated in Siger, pp. 26-81.

26. Gregory the Great asserted that Job himself was the author of the Book of Job (see *Moralia*, I, 15). For other exegetical opinions, see Datz, pp. 95-98, and Lewalski, pp. 12-13.

27. For Jerome's view, see the preface to his translation of Job, *PL*, XXXVIII, 1140 (cited by Lewalski, p. 13); and for the many authors who, down into the seventeenth century, repeat Jerome's observation about the hexameters of Job and go on to consider the poem's epic character, see Lewalski, pp. 13-17. One early dissenter from the view that Job is an epic was the fourth-century theologian Theodore of Mopsuestia, who thought that Job was modeled on the Greek dramas (see *PL*, LXVI, 697; cited in *Job*, ed. Pope, pp. xxx-xxxi). Another dissenter from the epic theory was the ninth-century poet and encyclopedist Rabanus Maurus, who described Job as a mixed drama-narrative (see *De universo*, *PL*, CXI, 420; cited and discussed by Siger, pp. 156-157). The view that Job is a drama was generally accepted by the mid-eighteenth century, or so one may infer from the primarily negative critical appraisal to which this view was subjected in an influential lecture by the then Oxford Professor of Poetry, Robert Lowth (rpt. in part in Glatzer, 1969, pp. 132-140). In the twentieth century the idea that the Book of Job has the form of a Greek tragedy was revived by Kallen, Walls, and others.

28. On the spread of the Office of the Dead and on related developments in the growth of the liturgy, see the essay by Edmund Bishop in *Prymer*, ed. Littlehales, esp. pp. xvi-xix. The history of Job in the liturgy is briefly surveyed by Hausen, pp. 28-32; Datz, pp. 167-171; and Siger, p. 29.

29. See Wyclif's "Of Feigned Contemplative Life," in *Fourteenth Century Verse and Prose*, ed. Sisam, pp. 119-128, esp. p. 123.

30. For this quotation from the Commendatio animae, see Siger, p. 29, who is citing *Liturgia romana vetus*, ed. Antonio Lodovico Muratori (Venice, 1748), I, 750; and for the text of the Office of the Dead, see n. 32, below.

31. The situation may soon be remedied, however. Now in progress, under the editorship of Knut Ottosen of the Institute of Church History at the University of Aarhus, is a "comprehensive catalogue of the responses and verses of the Office of the Dead gathered from every western diocese and monastery with a proper liturgy, and investigation of the origin and development of the office" (see Gioia, p. 181).

32. The edition of the Sarum Breviary to which I refer in the following discussion is *Breviarium ecclesiae Sarum*, ed. Procter and Wordsworth, which prints the Office of the Dead in vol. 2, cols. 271-282. On the special prominence of Sarum in the Western Church, see Bailey, *Processions of Sarum*, p. ix.

33. This is the plausible explanation offered by Bishop, in *Prymer*, ed. Littlehales, p. xxiii.

34. The text is reproduced from *Prymer*, ed. Littlehales, pp. 56-70. I have not indicated expanded abbreviations and have omitted the editor's footnotes. Chapter and verse are according to the Vulgate.

35. On Job's appearance in worm charms, see Pinto, pp. 44-59, 81-137. Dr. Pinto, who very kindly provided me with photocopies of the relevant portions of her dissertation, informs me that she is now preparing a book on Job in medieval European folk medicine.

36. Studied by Bouchard, Brody, Rollet, and others. Though the diagnoses they offer are for the most part fanciful, these scholars have gathered together and reproduced many illustrations that reveal how medieval people saw Job's physical suffering portrayed.

37. See Hausen, p. 31; and for recent "diagnosis" of Job's malady, see chapter 1, n. 19, above. In the Middle Ages it was often assumed that Job suffered from worms and leprosy (see Bouchard; Brody, pp. 48, 56; Lannois; Rollet; and Siger, pp. 69-71). In the seventeenth century, when many learned heads were bent over the Book of Job in an effort to diagnose Job's illness, one writer, Jeremiah Drexelius, advanced the notion that Job suffered from a whole battery of illnesses, including cancer, depression, elephantiasis, arthritis, worms, ulcers, colitis, nephritis, and insomnia (cited by Siger, p. 70).

38. See Bandmann, Lannois, and Meyer, for other examples.

39. There is significant mention of shrines of Saint Job in the pilgrimage narrative of Egeria (Etheria?), a fourth-century Spanish nun (see Egeria, *Journal*, ed. Pétré, pp. 46-48 and 147, n. 3). In their accounts of the Holy Land, Higden, Mandeville, and others also refer to shrines of Job. Also of interest, though it dates from the second half of the nineteenth century, is the account by Wetzstein of his visit to the medieval monastery of Job in Hauran, Syria, where—even at this late date—Job's tomb, his fountain, the stone on which he reclined, and pieces of rock said to be Job's hardened worms were venerated.

3. The Medieval Literary Heritage

1. Job figures briefly as an *exemplum patientiae* in the works of the ninth-century poets Milo of St. Amand, Wandalbert of Prüm, and Wala-

frid Strabo (see *MGH Poetae*, III, ii, 630; II, 585; and II, 295, respectively). Earlier in the Middle Ages, Job frequently appears alongside other Old Testament worthies, as in poems by Hilary of Poitiers or Venantius Fortunatus (for references and discussion, see Siger, pp. 205-212). On the appearance of Job in the works of Aldhelm and Bede, see n. 12, below.

2. For textual history and bibliography, see *Apocalypse*, ed. Hennecke and Schneemelcher, II, 755-759. In the following discussion, all citations of the *Apocalypse*—also known as Visio Pauli—are from this edition.

3. On the condemnation of the *Apocalypse*, its translation into various languages, and its subsequent influence, see *Apocalypse*, ed. Hennecke and Schneemelcher, II, 755-759; and Silverstein (1935), pp. 3-14, and Silverstein (1959).

4. The slim foundation for the story seems to have been 2 Corinthians 12:2-4, where Paul attributes a heavenly voyage to an unnamed acquaintance.

5. Cp. the appearance of Job in the following prayer for the ordination of a bishop, found in pseudo-Clementine, *Apostolical Constitutions*, which dates from around the same time as the *Apocalypse*: "[Thou] who hast fore-ordained priests from the beginning for the government of Thy people—Abel in the first place, Seth and Enos, and Enoch and Noah, and Melchisedeck and Job" (*ANCL*, XVII, 214-215).

6. See *Testament*, ed. Kohler, pp. 276-278.

7. *Founders of the Middle Ages*, p. 192. Citations of the *Psychomachia* in the following discussion are from the edition and translation by H. J. Thompson in the Loeb Classical Library (I have made a few slight changes in the parts of his translation I cite).

8. On Prudentius' popularity in the Middle Ages and the special prominence of the *Psychomachia*, see Prudentius, *Psychomachia*, ed. Lavarenne, pp. 22-26 and 58-78. For a recent study of the *Psychomachia*, see Smith, pp. 181-183, on the appearance of Job in the poem.

9. For Prudentius' possible indebtedness to the *Apocalypse*, consult *Apocalypse*, ed. Hennecke and Schneemelcher, II, 755.

10. For Prudentius' christological reading of the Abraham story, see *Psychomachia*, I, 274-279; and for examples of the christological interpretation of the Job story by some of Prudentius' contemporaries, see chapter 2, n. 18, above.

11. The biblical influence on Old English literature is treated by Cook, pp. xiii-lxxx, Morrell, and Shepherd. For the influence of the Apocrypha on Old English—a subject on which there is much more work still to be done—see Kaske, and Ogilvy, pp. 66-74. Incidental allusions to the Book of Job in Old English are listed in Cook, p. 326.

12. For lists of allusions to Job in the writings of Aldhelm and Bede, see *Aldhelmi Opera*, *MGH*, XV, 542; Bede, *Ecclesiastical History*, ed. Plummer, II, 392-394; and the indices to the not yet complete *Bedae Venerabilis Opera* in *Corpus Christianorum Series Latina*, vols. 118a-120 and 122. On the lost commentary on the Book of Job by Bede (?), see Vaccari.

13. References to *Ascension* (also known as *Christ II*) and the *Phoenix* are from the editions in *Exeter Book*, pp. 15-27 and 94-113, respectively.

14. The main source of *Ascension* is Gregory the Great's Twenty-ninth Homily on the Gospels. For an analysis of how Cynewulf has adapted the entire passage in Gregory to suit his ends, see Dubois, pp. 103-105; and for other putative allusions to Job in Cynewulf's poetry, see Dubois, p. 13, n. 3; p. 27, n. 5; p. 28, n. 8; and pp. 56-58.

The main source of the *Phoenix* is Lactantius' *De ave phoenice*, but the Job allusion is adapted from an obscure Job commentary, possibly by Philip the Presbyter (see *Phoenix*, ed. Blake, pp. 21-22).

15. For the triptych image see Anderson, p. 62. The unity and authorship of the so-called *Christ* poem are disputed (see Anderson, pp. 61-63).

16. See Besserman (1973[2]); and on Ælfric's general indebtedness to Gregory and other exegetes, see Ælfric, *Homilies*, ed. Pope, I, 150-177. My quotations and translations of the Job homily are from Ælfric, *Homilies*, ed. Thorpe, II, 446-460.

17. For a list of manuscripts of Ælfric's Job homily, see Ker, pp. 514-515; and for Middle English versions, see *Early English Homilies*, ed. Warner, pp. 123-129.

18. For editions of the two Old English poems entitled *Body and Soul*, see *Exeter Book*, pp. 174-178, and *Vercelli Book*, pp. 54-59, and see Kurtz, pp. 253-257.

19. See *Analecta Anglo-Saxonica*, ed. Thorpe, p. 10; and for scholarly opinions for and against Thorpe's thesis that the book of Job lies behind the *Riming Poem*, see Grubl, pp. 73-76.

20. Goldsmith's contention that the Book of Job influenced the *Beowulf* poet was anticipated, in a limited way, by Crawford.

21. Wolfe's comment is cited by Glatzer (1969), p. ix. Frye, p. 57.

22. The possibility, however, should not be dismissed out of hand. Clearly, there is still room for clarification of the generic and thematic affinities of these Old English poems, and the Book of Job may be of some use. For some recent suggestions about their affinities to wisdom literature, if not specifically to Job, see Bloomfield, "Understanding Old English Poetry," in *Essays*, pp. 59-80.

23. The works discussed in the following pages are selected from among a larger number. There are, for example, a number of Medieval German works which treat Job, including a complete paraphrase of the Book of Job, edited by Karsten. In addition, Hartmann von Aue's *Der Arme Heinrich* has striking affinities with the Job legend. For bibliography and discussion of these and other medieval works relevant to the history of the Job legend, see Datz and Wielandt.

An Italian poem on Job, *Historia de sancto Job propheta*, written about 1495 by Giuliano Dati of Florence, is to date unpublished. A medieval Portugese verse paraphrase of the Book of Job has recently been published by J. Mendes de Castro. (The last two works were called to my attention by Professors Giuseppe Bisaccia and Francis M. Rogers, respectively.)

24. Citations of "Liber Iob" in the following discussion are all from Beichner's edition, and the prose translations are my own. For other adaptations of the *Moralia*, see chapter 2, n. 24, above. Especially noteworthy

is Peter of Blois' *Compendium in Iob*, a kind of handbook for princes written at the direction of Henry II of England, when Peter was a clerk in the household of the Archbishop of Canterbury, and presented to the king in 1173. About a hundred years later the work was translated into Old French, in which form it came to be known as *L'Hystore Job*.

25. On the influence of the *Aurora*, see Peter Riga, *Aurora*, ed. Beichner, I, xxvii-xlvii.

26. Beichner fails to point out that there is a significant overlap between verses from the Book of Job on which Peter comments and the verses from Job in the Office of the Dead. The overlap includes Job 7:16, 21; 10:1, 20-22; 13:23-28; and 14:1-2, 4, 6.

27. Citations of the various versions of *Pety Iob* discussed below are from *Wheatley Manuscript*, ed. Day, pp. 59-64; *Twenty-Six Political and Other Poems*, ed. Kail, pp. 107-143; and *Prymer*, ed. Littlehales, pp. 56-70. For discussion of the language, manuscripts, and so on of the various versions and for relevant bibliography, see Severs, *Manual*, II, 383-384 and 536-537. See also the manuscripts transcribed and compared by M. Allen, pp. 362-401, and her discussion of Job and the liturgy, pp. 260-289. For the Old French *Paraphrase des IX leçons de Job*, also known as *Vigiles des morts*, see Pierre de Nesson, pp. 20-38, 71-106.

28. On Rolle's Latin *Job*, see H. E. Allen, pp. 130-144; and for arguments against attributing *Pety Iob* to Rolle, see H. E. Allen, pp. 369-370.

29. For the Adam/Jesus typology, see for example Luke 3:38, Romans 5:14, 1 Corinthians 15:22, 45. And for the self-comparison of Job with Adam, see Job 31:33 (a textual crux discussed in *Job*, ed. Pope, p. 238, n. 33a). On exegetical equations of Job with Adam and Jesus, see Gregory, *Moralia*, I, 138; II, 2; III, 677. And for further references, see chapter 2, n. 18, above. On the Job/Adam equation in Jewish tradition, see Glatzer, " 'Knowest Thou?'," pp. 78-84.

30. "But all those hardships which blessed Job undergoes it is not meet should be let pass in silence, and that the obscurity of ignorance should cover them from man's knowledge; for so many may be edified for the preserving of patience, as they who, by grace from above replenishing them, may be made acquainted with the achievements of his patience. And hence the same blessed Job would have the strokes which he feels carried into an example, in that he immediately adds, saying; Ver. 23, 24. '*O that my words were now written . . .*' " (*Moralia*, II, 157). See also Bruno of Asti, *Expositio*, *PL*, CXCVI, 618.

31. In the following discussion, citations from the Middle English metrical paraphrase of Job are from *A Middle English Metrical Paraphrase of the Old Testament*, ed. Kalén and Ohlander. My observations on the language, date, provenance, and sources of this Middle English Poem (hereafter referred to as *Paraphrase*) are derived from Kalén and Ohlander, I, iii-cxciv and IV, 5-7.

32. Severs, *Manual*, II, 382.

33. Kalén also mentions the possibility that the *Paraphrase* and the Old French poem both go back to a common source (I, clxxxii). For the case

against the influence of the Old French Job paraphrase on the Middle English poem, see M. Allen, pp. 347-361.

34. On the question of Job's nationality, see chapter 1, n. 6, above; and cp. the following comment by Gregory the Great: "to confound our shamelessness, a Gentile [Job] is handed down to be our example, that as he that is set under the Law disdains to pay obedience to the Law, he may at least be roused by comparing himself with him, who without the Law lived as by law" (*Moralia*, I, 17). For Nicholas of Lyra's repudiation of the view that Job was descended from Esau—a view which Nicholas rightly attributes to the mistaken identification of Job with Jobab—see *Postillae*, II, hhr (see also n. 47, below).

35. In the *Testament* Job learns that his afflictions stem from Satan even before their onset (see *Testament*, ed. Kraft, 3.1-5). Other similarities between the *Testament* and the *Paraphrase* are few, but there is at least one interesting, if slight, point of contact. When Job in the *Paraphrase* says: "ffor In þat otterest end / helpe forto neuyn is none / Ne medcyn þat may mend / bot þi mercy allon" (lines 15,165-15,168), we recall the following lines from the *Testament*, spoken by Job as he refuses aid from the physicians his comforters had brought with them: "My healing and treatment are from the Lord, who created even the physicians" (38.13b). The similarity between the two passages could be accidental, but it is also possible that the author of the *Paraphrase* was aware of the apocryphal tradition that Job turned down his comforters' offer of medical assistance. Not quite willing to add the physicians episode to the plot of the biblical story he was paraphrasing, he instead has Job disclaim any hope that medicine can help him.

36 For references to Lazarus in *Pety Iob*, see *Twenty-Six Political and Other Poems*, ed. Kail, p. 117, lines 311-312; and *Prymer*, ed. Littlehales, p. 60, lines 6-7. In this connection, it is interesting to note the existence of a postmedieval English carol about Job. The carol invokes Job as an *exemplum patientiae*, refers to the restitution of his wealth, and adduces Lazarus as a parallel case (*Oxford Book of Carols*, no. 60).

37. "Middle English Metrical Life of Job," ed. Garmonsway and Raymo, p. 77. All citations of the "Life of Job" in the following discussion are from this edition. For relevant bibliography, see Severs, *Manual*, II, 537.

38. See "Middle English Metrical Life of Job," ed. Garmonsway and Raymo, pp. 77-78 and, for a list of correspondences between verses in the poem and in the Vulgate, pp. 96-98. Unlike other vernacular works that treat Job, the "Life" was not influenced by the liturgy. References to the Vulgate are virtually all from chapters 1-2 and 42, the prose frame, and not from the verses which appear in the Office of the Dead. It is interesting to note that Francis Quarles, the best-known author of English emblem poetry, produced a work entitled *Iob Militant* (see Lewalski, pp. 107-108).

39. "Middle English Metrical Life of Job," ed. Garmonsway and Raymo, pp. 82-88; Hartt, 29-30; and Meiss, p. 68.

40. Severs, *Manual*, II, 384.

41. About Job's sacrifices after his childrens' feasts, Gregory writes: "The holy man knew that there can scarcely be feasting without offence; he

knew that the revelry of feasts must be cleansed away by much purification of sacrifices, and whatever stains the sons had contracted in their own persons at their feasts, the father wiped out by the offering of a sacrifice; for there are certain evils which it is either scarcely possible, or it may be said wholly impossible, to banish from feasting. Thus almost always voluptuousness is the accompaniment of entertainments; for when the body is relaxed in the delight of refreshment, the heart yields itself to the admission of an empty joy" (*Moralia,* I, 36).

42. Portraits of Job's wife as a stay rather than a stumbling block are infrequent but do occur, as in the *Testament of Job,* where she is a bit of both. In the Middle Ages mostly favorable portraits of Mrs. Job occur in *La Tour Landry,* pp. 103-104, and in the reference to Job's wife in Hermann von Fritzlar's poem on the Eustace legend (see Wielandt, pp. 89-90). For the most part, however, Job's wife was seen as Gregory and the other exegetes saw her (see chapter 2, n. 19, above).

43. Citations of *Pacience de Job* in the following pages are to the recent edition by Meiller, which is also my source for information about early editions, performances, and so on. For the Old French play about Job in *Le Mistère du Viel Testament,* a much shorter and simpler dramatic rendering of the Job legend, see the edition by Rothschild; and for a comparison of this play with *Pacience de Job,* see Meiller, p. 14, and further in Hausen, pp. 48-61. For a list of Italian, Latin, and Spanish plays about Job, see *Mistère du Viel Testament,* ed. Rothschild, V, x-xii.

44. See *Pacience de Job,* ed. Meiller, p. 408, n. Apr. 2757.

45. It is interesting to note that Gregory the Great took Job's three daughters to stand for the three theological virtues: Faith, Hope, and Charity (see *Moralia,* I, 57).

46. *Mimesis,* pp. 216-219. For antecedents and analogues of the diabolical council, the angel Michael's assault on Satan, and the devil's use of woman to deceive man, see the discussion and references in Murdoch, pp. 71-72. On Satan in Medieval Latin literature, see Alphandéry (which includes two or three interesting manifestations of the Job legend in the Latin Middle Ages).

47. The following gloss, from the beginning of the Book of Job in the Wycliffite Bible, reflects the variety of opinions about Job's lineage available to fourteenth-century English scholars: "Job was a very man in kynde, and his book is a very thing doon in dede, and not a parable, as sum men seiden. Job cam of Nacor, as Jerom, in the book of Ebreu Questiouns on Genesis, and Ebreis witnessen, to whiche it is to ȝyve credence in this matere; thouȝ Austyn and many othere seyn, that he cam of Abraham, bi Esau; also Job was the fyvethe from Abraham, and was in the tyme of Moyses" (II, 672). The information here probably derives from Nicholas of Lyra, *Postillae,* III, fol. 66v (cited by Siger, p. 37). The opinions of Jerome and Augustine that the glossator refers to are to be found in *Liber Hebraicarum quaestionum in genesim,* chap. 22, verses 20-22, in *PL,* XXIII, col. 1021; and *De civitate dei,* book 28, chap. 47, in *PL,* XLI, cols. 609-610. (See also chapter 1, n. 6; and chapter 3, n. 34.)

48. Harbage (*Annals,* pp. 28, 30, and 52) notes the existence of a lost

tragedy by Ralph Radcliffe (translator of More's *Utopia*?) entitled *De Iobi iusti afflictionibus* (c. 1550?); a lost biblical history by Robert Greene (?) entitled *Job* (c. 1590); and an anonymous lost biblical interlude entitled *Jube the Sane* [Job the Saint?] (c. 1550). Other plays based on the Job story, mostly modern or contemporary, are listed by Coleman.

49. All quotations and line references are from the editions of these plays in *Macro Plays*, ed. Eccles.

50. On the playwright's familiarity with the *Psychomachia*, see *Marco Plays*, ed. Eccles, p. xx.

51. D. M. Bevington, *From Mankind to Marlowe*, p. 48, as cited in *Macro Plays*, ed. Eccles, p. xlv.

52. These and other parallels between *Mankind* and Job are pointed out by Neuss, pp. 47-49.

53. There is an incomplete list of Chaucer's biblical references in *Chaucer*, ed. Skeat, VI, 381-384. For lists of Chaucer's references to Job, see M. Allen, pp. 339-345; Dillon, p. 29; and Landrum, pp. 43-57, 219. Numerous minor allusions to Job and the Book of Job in Middle English are listed by M. Allen, pp. 339-346; Smyth; and Besserman (1973[1]), pp. 177-213.

54. Ambrose of Milan and Gregory the Great both took Job 3:1 to be a pious shout of contemptus mundi and faith in the afterlife.

55. See Landrum, pp. 44-45. Severs located a fifteenth-century manuscript of the *De obedientia* which has a reference to Job at the point corresponding to lines 932-938, but this is far from conclusive evidence that the same passage was in Chaucer's source. The Latin reference to Job reads: "Verbumque beati Job compacientibus sibi respondit 'Dominus dedit, dominus obstulit; sicut domino placuit, ita factum est.' " Even if Chaucer had an earlier copy of this passage before him, he certainly elaborated upon it quite freely.

56. As Lillian Hornstein remarks: "Eustace (St. Eustace, Eustache, or Placidas), Constance, Florence, and Griselda themes . . . all emphasize the virtue of a meek Job-like faith" (Severs, *Manual*, I, 120). On the affinities between the legends of Eustace and Job, see Alphandéry, 892-893; Wielandt, pp. 96-100; and, most recently, Heffernan, pp. 72-73. For a list of medieval stories of this type, see Hornstein, in Severs' *Manual*, I, 120-132. The Eustace legend has been analyzed in great detail by Gerould and Heffernan.

Conclusion

1. Cited by Stanford, p. 1, from *Lives of the English Poets, Nicholas Rowe*, ed. G. B. Hill (Oxford, 1935), II, 68.

2. The history of Job from the Middle Ages to the present is a subject large enough for another book, or several. A few directions for further reading must suffice. On Job in the Renaissance, see Lewalski, Siger, and Wirszubski. Seventeenth-century uses of the legend, especially in epic poetry, are considered by Gossman, Hebaisha, Steadman, Stein, and Teunissen. On the eighteenth century and after, see Avni's bibliographic essays;

Besserman (1973[1]), pp. 215-252; Glatzer (1969); Hone, pp. 138-310; Levenson; Usmiani; and all of the essays in "Studies in the Book of Job," ed. Polzin and Robertson. Probably the most important adaptations of Job in the nineteenth century are in the prologue to Goethe's *Faust*, in Shelley's *Prometheus Unbound*, and in *Moby Dick* (for commentary, see Landsberger and Zhitlowsky; Damon and A. Wright; and N. Wright, respectively). Psychoanalytic interpretations of Job, besides Jung's more theological than psychological *Antwort auf Hiob*, have been advanced by Goitein and Reid.

3. *Praefatio in librum Job*, *PL*, XXVIII, 1081.

Index